Low maintenance Garden

Low maintenance Garden

Jenny Hendy

LONDON, NEW YORK, MUNICH, MELBOURNE, DELHI

SENIOR EDITOR Zia Allaway
SENIOR DESIGNER Rachael Smith
DESIGNER Alison Shackleton
EDITOR Caroline Reed
US EDITOR Christine Heilman
MANAGING EDITOR Anna Kruger
MANAGING ART EDITOR Alison Donovan
PICTURE RESEARCH Lucy Claxton, Mel Watson
PRODUCTION EDITORS Clare McLean, Jonathan Ward
PHOTOGRAPHY Peter Anderson

First American Edition, 2008
Published in the United States by
DK Publishing
375 Hudson Street
New York, New York 10014

RD145 March 2008
08 09 10 11   10 9 8 7 6 5 4 3 2

Published in Great Britain by Dorling Kindersley Limited.
A catalog record for this book is available from the Library
of Congress.

ISBN 978-0-7566-3343-1

DK books are available at special discounts when
purchased in bulk for sales promotions, premiums, fund-
raising, or educational use. For details, contact: DK
Publishing Special Markets, 375 Hudson Street, New York,
New York 10014 or SpecialSales@dk.com.

Printed and bound by Star Standard, Singapore

Discover more at
www.dk.com

Contents

Inspiring easy-care gardens

Outdoor spaces that require little maintenance can be as stylish and beautiful as those that need constant attention. The following pages showcase a selection of stunning designs, with ideas to tempt all tastes and for gardens large and small. Whether you want to create a chic urban courtyard, flowery meadow, or Zen-style gravel garden with just a few carefully placed plants, you will find inspiration on the following pages.

Design ideas for easy-care gardens

There are a great many reasons why you may want to make your yard easier and less time-consuming to maintain.

Happily, there are numerous strategies and solutions that can be employed without sacrificing aesthetics.

Pictures clockwise from left

Outdoor gallery The planting of a garden can be quite sparse if each specimen is chosen and sited with care, rather like an arrangement of sculptures. With a simple, uncluttered backdrop, this approach creates an opportunity to really appreciate the form and texture of the plants in your collection. Gravel laid over a weed-suppressing membrane provides a foil for the plants, and to keep the design interesting, aggregates can be enlivened with decorative paving, or cobbles and boulders. In this garden, large rocks anchor the planting and treated timbers, laid like stepping-stones, direct the eye to a circular mosaic feature with a striking contemporary container providing a focus in the center. Alternatively, you could use a self-contained water feature, such as a bubbling millstone.

Dining room Decking brings a roomlike quality and can be used to create a stylish outdoor dining area. This is especially valuable where space indoors is at a premium. To create a visually exciting design that requires very little upkeep, make sure the backdrop and planting around the deck are as simple as possible. A few bold color highlights and nighttime illumination will add designer sparkle.

Simple division Larger gardens designed for minimum maintenance are often best divided into a series of compartments. These can be partially screened from one another, or left open to enjoy the sense of space. To give each section its own character, and to add interest, try using contrasting landscape materials—on flat surfaces you can introduce changes in level, such as a raised deck or beds, or a sunken seating area. With a limited planting palette, it is important to be creative with flooring detail, and to include plenty of evergreens, such as the grasses (*Stipa tenuissima*) and sedges (*Carex*) used here.

Design ideas for easy-care gardens *continued*

Pictures clockwise from top left

Paved patio Small, enclosed spaces are perfect for paving—a low-maintenance, relatively weed-free alternative to grass. By planting in raised beds, narrow borders, and pots, you can maintain a range of plants that would satisfy even the most avid gardener. Spend time designing your garden, building in practical requirements as well as incorporating different textures and patterns to create interest. Here, cobbles and a ceramic water feature provide a focus, with hostas and bamboo adding an Asian note.

Mediterranean garden This swirling stuccoed wall, painted a dusty terra-cotta, suggests a garden built in a sunny climate. Slender Italian cypress, an old oil jar, and ironwork furniture strengthen the Mediterranean flavor. The wall is the right height to act as impromptu seating and, adding to the ambience, the air is filled with perfume from the white lilies, pink roses, and aromatic herbs.

Space for children Although children enjoy playing on lawns, other surfaces are more versatile. Little ones will enjoy a sandbox (covered when not in use), and varying the flooring materials and incorporating changes in level can create opportunities for play. A splinter-free deck suits bare feet and the level surface is ideal for a variety of toys and activities. Choose robust plants, such as the phormium, grasses, and bamboos in this child-friendly garden.

Raised beds As well as providing easy-access planting spaces, raised beds are design features in their own right. They also offer casual seating and welcome changes in level in otherwise flat, featureless spaces. This bed, with its curved dry-stone walling effect, provides ideal, sharply-drained conditions for a wide range of hardy alpines.

Formal design

An ordered or symmetrical garden, with a combination of simple geometric shapes, inspires a feeling of calm. The style is adaptable, and it is easy to create stunning vistas and dramatic focal points.

Pictures clockwise from top left

Creating a focus The elements of this charming little garden are simple and unfussy, yet because of the strong central axis guiding the eye down the narrow pathway, the effect is quite theatrical. Tall *Verbena bonariensis* are neatly enclosed by clipped, dwarf boxwood hedging, which, being evergreen, provides a strong architectural framework, even in the depths of winter. A traditional brick path opens out into a circular paving feature with a large Greek pot at its center, but this could be replaced by a pebble mosaic or an eye-catching piece of sculpture.

Elegant dining Although most often associated with grand historic properties, a formal touch, utilizing symmetry, works in a variety of situations and can make a previously ordinary space look stunning. Here, French windows open out onto a raised deck used for dining. Elevated views of the garden are framed by tall, stylish containers filled with lavender, and a grapevine-covered pergola. The formality continues with matching steps, clipped boxwood edging, and twin potted marguerites.

Contemporary twist There's no reason why you can't take elements of Renaissance gardens and use them to add style to a contemporary space. Here, tall perennials (*Miscanthus* and *Rudbeckia*) are contained by low evergreen hedging—just like a modern-day parterre— and clipped topiary in matching terra-cotta pots makes a stylish statement. A rill or narrow canal set into the deck would also work well.

Mirror image This study in symmetry and minimalism has created a garden that is extremely easy to maintain. Simply planted, the design succeeds by clever stage-setting. The onlooker's eye is drawn to the water curtain sculpture by a line of cube-shaped box topiaries running along the central axis. Meanwhile, the two formal white containers, matching raised beds planted with bamboo, and the arching tree branches frame the view perfectly. Keep the surfaces immaculate to avoid visual distractions.

Contemporary creations

Modern minimalism has much to offer busy garden owners. Simple layouts, easily maintained hard landscaping, and color and interest that don't rely solely on planting are useful elements often exploited by contemporary designers.

Pictures clockwise from far left

Color impact Use bold shades, like purple or red, to enhance contemporary designs and create exciting backdrops. Here, architectural foliage plants, including phormium and eucalyptus, are all the more striking against the painted fence. A stuccoed wall could also act as a modern minimalist canvas, if painted with masonry paint.

Sculptural focus The gleaming white spiral of this art installation stands out dramatically against the dark uncluttered backdrop and restrained planting plan. Alternative sculptural elements, such as a large container or fountain, could be used to create a focal point strong enough to carry the simple design.

Restrained planting While gardens often rely on colorful flowers and foliage for interest, you can still create an attractive outdoor space using a limited planting palette. This ground plan is well defined, and strengthened by innovative flooring and dividing walls. Only a few of the rectangular compartments contain plants—many are filled with water and bridged by decking walkways.

Novel materials You can achieve contemporary effects with high-tech materials. Consider acrylic plastic panels, or polished and galvanized metal sheeting for facing walls and edging beds, and metal grids for flooring. Here, corrugated metal contains a grass-filled border.

Simple composition Taking inspiration from Zen gardens, this simple but effective layout, with a background of white stone chips and black trellises, features a single phormium surrounded by carefully selected rocks and a black glazed sphere.

Havens for wildlife

Low-maintenance gardens can be surprisingly wildlife friendly. Many easy-care plants attract bees and butterflies, and shrubs and trees with ornamental fruits offer a feast for birds.

Pictures clockwise from top left

Watering hole Providing a safe vantage point to drink and bathe, a birdbath can become a hive of activity for birds; site conveniently, as you'll need to top it off regularly. To avoid problems with cats, plant around the base with low ground cover. Here, blue fescues (*Festuca*), houseleeks (*Sempervivum*), and sedums are used. A shallow-sided pebble pool would also attract amphibians and dragonflies.

Carefree meadow One way to reduce the need for regular mowing in a large garden, while increasing wildlife potential, is to convert sections of formal lawn into wildflower meadows. On poor, sandy soil, you can establish a meadow using wildflower plugs and bulbs suitable for naturalizing. More reliable results are achieved by removing sod with a sod-cutting machine and then re-sowing with a perennial wildflower mix (*see pp.78–79*).

Insect attractors Beneficial hoverflies seek out single-flowered, hardy summer annuals, such as *Eschscholzia* and *Limnanthes*, and bees love blue flowers like this California bluebell (*Phacelia campanularia*). *Verbena bonariensis* and *Buddleja davidii* are magnets for bees and butterflies. For the first insects of the season, plant sunny gravel or raised beds with spring alpines—alyssum, arabis, aubrietia, heathers, grape hyacinth (*Muscari*), and crocus.

Bird cover Large evergreen and deciduous shrubs, dense hedges, and trees are vital for birds. They not only need safe nesting and nighttime roosting sites, but also places to shelter during bad weather and to escape airborne predators. Without cover nearby, birds are nervous about entering a garden, even one with feeders.

Berry banquet Provide a wide range of fruiting and berrying plants, with some ripening in late summer and others ready for harvest well into winter. This long-lasting buffet will cater to local birds as well as visiting migrants. Low ground-cover plants such as *Cotoneaster salicifolius* 'Gnom' (*illustrated*), wall shrubs like pyracantha, roses with large colorful hips, and small ornamental trees, such as rowans (*Sorbus*) and crab apples (*Malus*), are ideal.

Courtyard gardens

Textures and colors are viewed close up in these intimate spaces, so choose materials and plants for maximum effect. Also include some shade and water, as well as lighting for evenings outside.

Pictures clockwise from top left

Big, bold pots Some outdoor spaces are completely paved, but you can grow almost any plant in a container—provided it is big enough—including small trees, elegant bamboos and grasses, a wide range of shrubs and climbers, as well as perennials, bulbs, and ferns. This pot contains *Nandina domestica*, purple cordyline, heuchera, and trailing ivy. Evergreens help the garden look good all year, and courtyards often have a sheltered microclimate, allowing less hardy species to be grown. Install automatic irrigation to make light work of watering.

Tranquil oasis This striking, contemporary walled garden has a Moorish feel. The lush planting, inspired by a rich purple and cerise color palette, features a glowing *Cercis canadensis* 'Forest Pansy' in the corner, and a large formal pool with "floating" stepping-stones. The arbor-covered, paved terrace juts out over the surface, taking you right to the water's edge.

Hot property Courtyards can feel gloomy if surrounded by high walls, but you can lift the atmosphere and create more light by applying color (on taller walls, just paint to a line above the ground-floor windows). Here, a vibrant orange has been used on a curved wall, contrasting with beds of Mediterranean herbs, perennials, and grasses. Where shade is a problem, whitewashed walls may appear to be the answer, but these need frequent touching up and white can seem harsh in a cool climate; instead, try light pink, pale green, watery blue, or pearly gray. Also consider wall-mounted mirrors or reflective metal panels, murals and *trompe l'oeil* (illusory 3-D effects) or, for a historic look, decorative trellis panels.

Garden café Courtyards can be transformed into an extra room for your house, and an *al fresco* dining room or outdoor kitchen can be used in fine weather at any time of year. Raise or sink the dining area to give it definition, and construct screens with giant pots or raised beds filled with architectural evergreens, like the cordyline and clipped boxwood balls in this stylish garden.

New-wave planting

This impressionistic style of gardening, sometimes known as prairie planting, uses harmonious combinations of herbaceous perennials and ornamental grasses to create naturalistic and long-lasting displays.

Pictures clockwise from top left

Planting philosophy Choose easy-care perennials that don't need deadheading, staking, or frequent division. Plants that have everlasting flowers or sculptural seedheads in fall and winter are particularly useful; most grasses, even deciduous types, retain foliage and diaphanous seedheads through winter. For the prairie look, plant swaths of single cultivars and punctuate with isolated clusters. Soften the effect of heavier flower and foliage forms by using airy flower stems and billowing grasses, and vary the height of plants to create interesting undulations. Here, crimson astrantia rise above a ribbon of erigeron interspersed by tussocks of *Stipa tenuissima*.

Stylized nature Planted *en masse*, color-restricted displays of flowering perennials and grasses produce a stylized, contemporary version of a meadow. Here, raised beds lift the planting to create a feeling of enclosure around this outdoor dining area. An elegant mixture of tall miscanthus grasses and *Verbena bonariensis* opens up to reveal blocks of lavender on the opposite side.

Lingering effects From midsummer onward, *Rudbeckia fulgida*, as well as plants like the heleniums and achilleas seen growing here, put on a long-lasting show. Interspersed with hardy grasses—such as calamagrostis, miscanthus, panicum and stipa—they knit together seamlessly, covering the ground and preventing weed growth. Many of the grasses also flower in late summer, adding to the display, and the foliage fades to biscuit or develops red and purple hues as fall approaches. It is only necessary to cut back hard when growth begins again in spring.

Grassy retreat The planting in this gravel garden is relaxed and informal—the seating area is completely cocooned by billowing grasses, and narrow pathways wind lazily through the subtle planting. Although there are few colored blooms, this garden will change throughout the year and will look magical with a dusting of frost.

Creating your garden

Before making final plans for your garden, think about how much time you have to spare, and whether your designs will suit your lifestyle. You can then use the advice in this chapter to help you to choose hard landscaping materials, lawns and other soft surfaces, and water features. Also included are step-by-step instructions showing how to build a few simple garden structures, such as a path, raised bed, and deck.

Benefits of a low-maintenance garden

With adjustments to your existing yard, or strategic planning when building from scratch, you can enjoy a beautiful garden even if you have little time or energy to look after it. Most high-maintenance plants and plans have low-maintenance alternatives, and many routine jobs can be omitted altogether.

Who needs a low-maintenance garden?

We simply do not have as much time as we used to, and yet the garden is increasingly seen as a sanctuary and an antidote to modern living. Whether you are pursuing a career, working odd shifts, spending hours commuting, or raising a young family, you will need to find a way to manage your garden more easily.

New gardeners may lack confidence in their abilities and want to start simply, and some homeowners are not particularly interested in the practical side of gardening, yet still appreciate and desire an attractive outdoor space. Older gardeners may find they no longer have the physical strength and energy to cultivate in the way they used to or, adopting a more carefree lifestyle, might be too busy traveling to garden regularly. And if you are a landlord with rental properties, you may only be able to visit them a few times a year.

Creative design and planting will ensure that ultra easy-care gardens like this urban yard are attractive, practical, and never boring.

With easy-care gardening strategies in place, you can cut down on regular or seasonal chores like raking leaves and lawn maintenance.

How much time do you have?

When designing your yard, first think about how frequently you will have time to maintain it.

Weekends If you have a few hours on the weekend, you may only have time to mow the lawn, do a little deadheading and tidying, and perhaps do some hand-weeding, hoeing, or hedge-trimming. Drought-tolerant shrubs and flowers in pots will survive with weekly waterings.

Once a month Lawns are not a good idea if you can only tackle gardening tasks once a month. Instead, replace them with paving, decking, or gravel. Reduce deadheading and pruning with a selection of easy-care plants, and install an automatic watering system.

A few times a year Gardening only once in a while restricts your options, so choose a combination of low-maintenance plants and hard landscaping. You can then limit jobs to tidying borders, cutting back old growth on perennials in late winter, and occasionally pruning overgrown trees and shrubs.

Time-saving tips

Watering Select drought-tolerant specimens, and plant in fall or spring to cut down the need to water while the roots are establishing. Set up pots with automatic irrigation.

Fertilizing Mulch with manure in late winter to keep the soil fertile. Once or twice a year, fertilize flowering plants, including those in containers, using a slow-release fertilizer.

Deadheading Choose plants with ornamental seedheads and avoid any that need deadheading to keep them blooming. Tidy ground-cover perennials and lavenders with shears.

Weeding Cover the ground with a weed-suppressing fabric camouflaged with gravel. Spray weeds with systemic weedkiller to kill the roots. Avoid soil disturbance and self-seeding plants.

Mowing Choose an easy-care grass seed mix. Reduce the lawn size and buy an efficient mower. Install a brick mowing strip next to borders and walls to eliminate edging.

Pruning Choose evergreens, as they rarely need pruning, and plants that only need one trim per year, such as *Buddleja davidii*. Avoid overly vigorous shrubs and allow plants room to grow.

Low- and high-maintenance ingredients

Choose the plants and materials in your garden carefully to minimize the workload.

Easy-care gardens

Paved or decked surfaces are easy to keep clean and weed-free, and surrounding your plants with hard landscaping, or growing them in raised beds, keeps them within bounds; you can also carry out most jobs in nearly any weather. Although there is an excellent selection of low-maintenance flowering shrubs and perennials, choosing specimens for their architectural qualities, foliage color, and texture, rather than for their blooms, will ensure that the planting is interesting year-round.

Hardy bulbs Dwarf and low-growing hardy bulbs, like crocus, scillas, and small daffodils, offer a maintenance-free spring show. For summer, plant alliums and low-growing lilies that do not need staking. Dying down gracefully, these bulbs are left in the ground to come up year after year.

Drought-busters Plants like these houseleeks do not need watering at all. If you live in a dry region, or the garden has a hot, sunny exposure and free-draining soil, focus on drought-tolerant plants, such as succulents or silver-leaved varieties. Avoid pots or consider installing automatic irrigation.

Plant-free features Bringing color into the garden with painted walls or trellises reduces the need for bright bedding displays. Decorative paving elements, such as pebble mosaics, add textural interest, while sculpture and stylish outdoor furniture provide maintenance-free highlights.

Labor-intensive gardens

Manicured lawns require a lot of upkeep: mowing and edging, weeding and feeding, moss-killing, scarifying to remove dead material, aerating to improve drainage, and sweeping up leaves in fall. Of course, a roughly maintained family lawn, or one where clover and other attractive "weeds" are allowed to grow, needs much less attention. Traditional borders full of blooms, and backed by flower-festooned walls and fences, look spectacular in summer, but it is difficult to keep on top of deadheading, staking, weeding, and watering, not to mention tying climbers and wall shrubs onto their supports. Self-seeding can also become a time-consuming problem.

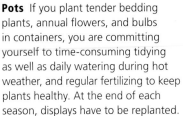

Pots If you plant tender bedding plants, annual flowers, and bulbs in containers, you are committing yourself to time-consuming tidying as well as daily watering during hot weather, and regular fertilizing to keep plants healthy. At the end of each season, displays have to be replanted.

Fast-growing hedge One of the most challenging tasks is keeping on top of quick-growing plants, like privet and tall conifers. Several cuts a year are required to maintain a neat profile and control height and spread, and removing the clippings can also be laborious.

Tender plants A recent trend in patio gardening has seen an increase in the use of exotics, such as bananas, tree ferns, cannas, and agaves. These plants are too large and expensive to discard at the end of summer, but need to be fully protected from frost *in situ* or in a glasshouse.

Assessing your site

Look critically at your yard before carrying out any major changes. Weigh up the pros and cons of features before removing them, and remember that mature, established plants may need less maintenance than new ones.

Which way does your yard face? Work out where the sun rises (east) and sets (west). Eastern exposures are sunny in the morning—winter and spring-flowering shrubs are vulnerable to frost here. West-facing walls and fences have sun in the afternoon and evening—ideal for relaxing after work. Areas in sun for much of the day are south-facing, and shady, cool spots opposite have a northern exposure.

What do you need?

Make a list of the various activities and areas planned for your yard, including places for growing plants, supporting wildlife, relaxing, cooking, and dining *al fresco*. Bear in mind factors like sun and shade, drainage, shelter from wind, and proximity to water and electrical outlets. Don't forget practicalities like easy access to garbage cans or recycling bins and compost piles, as well as storage space for garden tools and furniture.

Guinea pigs and rabbits like to graze and run on grass; lawns also benefit songbirds.

Make children's gardens versatile, and easy to adapt when they tire of play equipment.

Areas for outdoor entertaining might include a grill, a sunken fire pit, or a gazebo.

Understanding climate

You can live in an area that suffers from early and late frosts or that's battered by winds, while enjoying milder conditions in your garden. South- and west-facing yards are suntraps; walls and paving absorb daytime heat and radiate it back at night, keeping surrounding areas frost-free. Trees and hedges act as buffers against wind but, conversely, buildings can cause damaging turbulence. Such local variations are known as microclimates.

As sunny walls radiate heat, tender plants like this ceanothus can thrive in frosty regions.

Hedges and shrub borders slow the wind and provide shelter for plants and people.

Cold air pools at the bottom of slopes, and plants here are more vulnerable to frosts.

Boundaries and garden dividers

The style and fabric of the elements you choose to enclose or separate parts of your yard have a major impact on the overall effect of the garden. Boundary materials frequently act as a foil, but can also make a bold statement.

Wooden fence Choose the highest-quality fencing that you can afford for long-lasting results. Pressure-treated posts are easier to replace and last longer if placed into metal sockets rather than directly into concrete.

Trellis A decorative screening material with panels in various styles, a trellis may also include shaped pieces for special features. Letting in more light but offering less privacy than solid paneling, it is best for internal divisions.

Willow or hazel hurdles These hand-woven panels are perfect for cottage-style gardens. For a contemporary look, attach to aluminum posts or a solid lumber frame. Panels last for about eight years.

Stucco wall Cinder-block walls are quicker and cheaper to build than brick and, when stuccoed, can be painted in a range of colors to create a smart and stylish finish. Stucco is often used for contemporary designs.

Brick wall Garden walls are decorative and practical, and frostproof bricks are available in a range of styles to match adjacent buildings. Antique or reclaimed bricks create the illusion of age and are ideal for historic gardens.

Green dividers

Fences and walls provide opportunities to grow a wide variety of climbers and wall shrubs, and the plants help to camouflage boundary imperfections. Also, living screens of tall ornamental grasses, bamboos, shrubs, and trees offer exciting alternatives to formal hedging.

Bamboo screen Some bamboos make beautiful evergreen screens, which suit both Asian-style and contemporary yards. Non-invasive, clump-forming cultivars of *Phyllostachys* and *Fargesia* are ideal, their upright canes often developing attractive tints and banding. Plant a row in moisture-retentive ground, allowing them room to spread sideways. To control the width of the screen, remove unwanted bamboo shoots at ground level in late spring. Periodically thin out some mature canes, and remove leafy growth from the lower half of the screen.

Climbers There are only a few climbers that are self-clinging and do not require wires or trellis. These include *Hydrangea anomala* subsp. *petiolaris* (*above*) and ivy. Be sure to choose the right plant for the site and soil type—some prefer cool shade, while others bloom best on a sunny wall. Also consider the plant's ultimate height and vigor, to avoid problems in the future.

Yew hedge When clipped formally, this dark evergreen forms a dense wall or plain backdrop for borders. Relatively slow-growing, it can eventually be trained into arches and other pieces of green architecture. Yew is long-lived and regenerates from old wood if pruned hard. Although shade-tolerant, hedges are best cut wide at the base and narrow at the top, so that light falls evenly on the foliage.

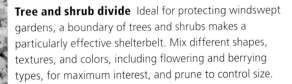

Tree and shrub divide Ideal for protecting windswept gardens, a boundary of trees and shrubs makes a particularly effective shelterbelt. Mix different shapes, textures, and colors, including flowering and berrying types, for maximum interest, and prune to control size.

Living willow screen In heavy clay soil, willow stems pushed into the ground will root easily. Setting these hardwood cuttings at an angle forms the beginning of a diamond lattice. Simply hook the willow stems under and over one another to the desired height, and then weave the excess at right angles to secure the upper edge of the screen. Trim the stems as necessary.

Fedge This is a cross between a fence and a hedge, and is an ingenious way to camouflage ugly chain-link fencing. It is best to use a plain green ivy for rapid cover and to produce a slim, dense, hedgelike structure. Plant pots of young, vigorous ivies at the base of the screen, and weave the shoots in and out as they grow. Once the fence is covered, trim the ivy using hand shears.

Selecting landscape materials

The natural or synthetic products you choose, and the patterns and designs you employ, make a big difference to the overall look of the garden. Other considerations include the cost of materials, ease of laying or installation, and long-term durability.

Granite pavers These hard-wearing cubes of granite are ideal for driveways and areas in heavy use, and can be arranged to make very attractive circular, curving, or interlocking paving patterns as well as the straightforward grid design illustrated. Made of natural stone, these paving blocks suit historic properties and country residences, but they can also be used in a variety of situations to add textural interest to areas paved with slabs. Granite pavers are expensive but concrete substitutes are available.

Using contractors When hiring someone to carry out hard landscaping work, be prepared to show them a scale drawing or at least mark out the areas to be paved or decked to avoid confusion. Get a number of quotes and, especially if the contractor hasn't been personally recommended, ask to see examples of their work so that you can do your own quality check. After considering your ideas, contractors may help you select suitable materials and provide paving samples; also discuss clearing and preparing the ground, waste removal, drainage requirements, electrical wiring, and paving patterns and designs. Once you are happy with a quote, draw up a formal agreement for the contractor to sign, stating exactly what you expect them to do for the price, with start and end dates.

Natural stone Ethically sourced sandstone, limestone, and granite paving reveals subtle colors when wet and does not chip or fade, but it tends to be thicker, heavier, and less uniform, and is more expensive than concrete reproductions. Consider hiring an experienced paving contractor.

Concrete paving There is a wide range of concrete paving available, from plain, contemporary designs to textured stone reproductions and modular paving sets. Quality varies, and some styles are thicker and more hardwearing with better resistance to chipping or fading in sunlight.

Woodstone A convincing substitute for wooden landscape timbers, the concrete is imprinted with the texture of weathered, reclaimed wood and suits country or cottage garden situations. It can also be used for steps, stepping stones in gravel, and to construct low raised flower beds.

Wooden decking Decking is warm underfoot and dries rapidly after rain. Do not use in shady areas as it quickly develops slippery algae. Off-the-shelf kits are available from do-it-yourself stores, but hire a specialist for larger, more complex areas. Western red cedar is naturally rot-resistant.

Sod New gardens are often laid with sod prior to implementing a design. A well-maintained lawn makes an attractive foil for borders and contrasts well with hard landscaping. Lawns are important for many birds and provide a safe play surface for children. Install a mowing edge.

Bricks Frostproof bricks, engineering bricks, and pavers can be laid in a wide variety of patterns, such as curving shapes and circular designs; they also add texture to areas paved with slabs. Bricks come in different shades and styles, including antique effects that suit older properties.

Cobbles Pebbles and cobbles of different colors and grades can be used with other materials, such as slate shards and tile fragments, to create paving mosaics like the circular feature above. Simple designs are not difficult to make, as the pebbles are bedded into a dry mortar.

Gravel This versatile and inexpensive material comes in many different grades and colors, allowing it to blend with other landscape materials. Laid over a permeable membrane, it's an easy way to create pathways and patios. Contain gravel to separate it from soil using slightly raised edgings.

Decorative aggregates Slate chips (*above*) are one of several stone aggregates now available for garden landscapes. More dramatic or contemporary effects can be created with colored stone chips and glass chips. Lay as for gravel, over a permeable membrane.

Designing with different materials

Hard surfaces act as a framework around which plants can grow and mature. The chosen material, and the style in which it is laid, can enhance the design of your outdoor space.

Decking jetty This substantial wooden platform hangs over the pool below, allowing close access to the water. The clean lines and restrained planting combine to create an open expanse of warm wood and tranquil water.

Basketweave bricks This garden is paved in a traditional design that suits older properties and has cottage-garden appeal. The weathered terra-cotta coloring and intricately textured surface of the bricks give an aged quality.

Sleek slabs Smooth, simple concrete pavers laid in a uniform row or geometric grid create a contemporary feel. This minimalist style of paving helps to emphasize the planting as well as architectural and design features.

Vintage stone Reclaimed stone from architectural salvage companies gives a garden a feeling of permanence. The worn and weathered surface of the stone adds character, perfect for this formal pool terrace edged in boxwood.

Zen gravel garden Gravel is used here to emulate a dry Zen garden or *karesansui*. The rugged boulders and simple evergreen plantings represent islands in a sea or lake, reflecting traditional Japanese designs.

How to lay paving slabs

Areas of paving will have a professional finish, provided you do the groundwork properly. Modern concrete slabs are much more manageable than larger stone pavers. Pick your patio design carefully to minimize cutting.

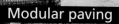

Modular paving

Many circular patio features come with all the pieces precut and ready for assembly. You can also buy squaring-off kits that allow circular features to be laid within a larger area paved with slabs.

1 Dig down to accommodate the slab depth, crushed stone, and mortar base, and ensure that the finished level is slightly below the sod. Line with treated lumber and check that the corners are absolutely square. Adjust so that the patio slopes away from the house at a gradient of 1:50.

2 Fix the lumber with pegs from the outside, nailing them into position from the inside; attach lines to the pegs to allow for checking depths. Fill with a 4-in (10 cm) layer of crushed stone and rake it level. Compact using a rented plate vibrator or compactor and recheck levels.

3 Starting in the corner, lay a bed of mortar for the first slab ¾–1¼ in (2–3 cm) deep, or use four or five blobs of mortar to support the slab. Lay the slab and tap gently into position using a rubber mallet. Insert wooden spacers between slabs for the mortared joints. Repeat for all slabs.

4 Use a level to check the levels and to maintain the fall away from the house. Leave mortar to dry for 24 hours and don't walk on the paving. If rain is forecast, cover the area with plastic sheeting. Once the base mortar has set, work more mortar into the joints using a pointing trowel.

How to lay gravel over a membrane

Separating the soil from a top layer of gravel using either landscaping fabric or a permeable membrane will ensure that the area remains relatively weed-free, and looks decorative too.

1 Dig over the area selected for your gravel garden, incorporating plenty of grit and compost to improve the soil quality and create good drainage. Level off with a rake to get rid of any undulations on the surface.

2 With assistance, spread the membrane over the ground, taking care not to contaminate the surface with soil. Bury the edges securely beneath brick edging, paving, or landscape timbers. If necessary, cement into position.

3 Generously overlap adjoining sheets of membrane and pin securely. This prevents the cut edges from curling up and fraying, and also stops perennial weeds from pushing through the seams.

4 Pour gravel, glass, or slate chips onto the membrane, spacing the piles regularly. Use a rake to distribute the aggregate evenly, ensuring that all of the membrane is covered to a depth of about 1 in (2.5 cm).

How to lay bricks on sand

The illustrated technique can be used to lay any simple, straight-sided area of frostproof bricks or pavers. For a curved path, contain the pavers within an edging of bricks laid on a bed of mortar.

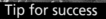

Tip for success

To do a really professional job of bedding in the bricks, you could rent a compactor or plate vibrator. This efficiently works the sand down between each of the pavers.

1 Dig out a channel deep enough for a brick and 2 in (5 cm) of sand. Edge with treated lumber and hold in place using wooden stakes. Ram the soil down with a batten until it is compact, then level with a layer of sharp sand.

2 Lay the bricks or pavers onto the sand bed. Laying them lengthwise (*see picture opposite*) reduces the need to cut so many bricks. Check that the bricks are perfectly level as you work using a long level.

3 Pour fine, kiln-dried sand over the finished pathway. This should be worked into the seams between the bricks to help stabilize them while allowing rainwater to soak through. There is no need to use cement mortar.

4 Work the sand into the seams using a broom or hand brush. Allow the path to settle for a few days, then go over the surface once more with sand, filling any gaps.

How to build a deck from a kit

A small raised deck can add emphasis and design flair to an area of your garden, as this chic corner patio shows. With the aid of some basic power tools, most do-it-yourself deck kits are reasonably easy to construct.

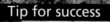

Tip for success

When you want a curved edge, place the decking boards diagonally on the frame. Use a pencil and string tied to a nail to draw a smooth curve across the boards. Cut with a power saw and treat the edge with preservative.

1 Lay out the four bearers to form a square frame and butt-join them at the corners using 6 in (15 cm) wood screws. Mark off equally spaced fixing points for the central struts, then attach them to the frame, screwing in from the outside.

2 Remove a deck-sized area of sod. Position a paving slab under each corner of the frame, midway down each side, and in the center, beneath the struts. Mark around the slabs, then remove them and dig out 1 in (2.5 cm) of topsoil, replacing it with gravel. Replace the slabs and check levels.

3 Lay membrane over the slabs, then cut around them until only the soil is covered. Pour gravel around the slabs to leave a weed-free finish. Put the frame in place, then position the first board along the edge of the deck and fix into the frame using decking screws.

4 Continue laying the boards, screwing into the struts below and leaving small gaps in between, according to instructions, so that you won't need to cut the final board along its length. Cover the edge of the framework with a fascia of treated lumber.

How to make a raised bed and mowing edge

A sturdy timber-framed raised bed is quick and easy to construct, especially if the pieces are precut to length at a lumberyard. If your bed is adjacent to a lawn, finish it off neatly with a simple brick mowing edge.

1 Dig out strips of sod wide enough to accommodate the timbers. Pressure-treated landscape timbers are an economical alternative to rot-resistant hardwoods like oak. You could also consider buying reclaimed hardwood.

2 Lay the timbers out *in situ* and check that they are level using a long level, or a plank of wood supporting a shorter level. Check the levels diagonally between timbers, as well as along their length.

3 Ensure that the base is square by checking that the diagonals are equal in length. For a perfect square or rectangular bed, it is a good idea to have the timbers precut to size at the lumberyard.

How to make a raised bed *continued*

4 Using a rubber mallet, gently tap the wood so that it butts up against the adjacent piece; it should stand perfectly level and upright according to the readings on your level. Remove soil as necessary.

5 Drill through the end timbers into the adjacent pieces at both the top and bottom to accommodate a couple of long, heavy-duty coach screws. Screw firmly into position, securing the base ready for the next level to be built.

6 Arrange the next set of timbers, making sure that these overlap the joints below to give the structure added strength. Check with a level before screwing in the final set of fasteners, as for Step 5.

7 For the extra drainage required by tender plants, such as Mediterranean herbs or alpines, partially fill the base with rubble or stone chips. Then add sifted topsoil that is guaranteed free of perennial weeds.

How to make a mowing edge

1 Using a spare brick to measure the appropriate distance, set up a line of string to act as a guide. Dig out a strip of sod deep enough to accommodate the bricks plus 1 in (2.5 cm) of mortar.

2 Lay a level mortar mix in the bottom of the trench as a foundation for the bricks. Set them on top, leaving a small gap between each brick. Although this design is straight, mowing edges can also be placed around curves.

3 With a level, check that the bricks are aligned and slightly below the surface of the sod; use a rubber mallet to gently tap them into position. Once set in place, you will be able to mow straight over the bricks.

4 Finally, use a dry mix to mortar the joints between the bricks, working the mixture in with a trowel. Clean off the excess. The mowing edge makes maneuvering the mower easier, and minimizes the need to trim.

Water feature options

Water is an invaluable asset. It brings movement, sound, and a relaxed mood to the garden, and a simple pool or sparkling fountain will brighten up areas of hard landscaping.

Bubble pool The gentle movement created by a single jet of water, set to just break the surface, lends a tranquil feel to this formal walled parterre. Atmospheric moisture helps to concentrate aromatic oils released by the herbs.

Letterbox fountain This clever arrangement of wall cascades, culminating in a narrow curtain, intensifies the effect of the water. It could fit into the smallest of yards, and lit at night would provide an enchanting focus.

Rills Offering a mere glimpse of water, these narrow channels carry moving water that glints through the garden. They magically disappear beneath paving, only to reappear, feeding into a pool or pebble fountain.

Reflecting pool Still water acts like a mirror, reflecting the surrounding plants and ever-changing skies. If made sufficiently deep, planted with oxygenating plants, and kept free of leaves, these pools are relatively easy to maintain.

Themed water feature This Japanese *tsukobai*, modeled on a traditional design, emphasizes the Asian courtyard theme. The trickling water is soothing and, as the reservoir is hidden, it is also child-friendly.

Setting up a low-maintenance water feature

Once assembled, water features that run from a hidden reservoir, like this elegant bubble pool, require no more than an occasional top-off with water. Unlike garden ponds, they take up very little room and are safe for children.

1 Dig a hole large enough to accommodate the water reservoir that will be positioned below the bubble pool. These can be bought as part of a complete kit from most water-garden outlets and large garden centers.

2 Wearing thick gloves, remove sharp stones from the wall of the hole and then line with damp sand to provide a cushioning layer. Compact the sand with your hands, then install the reservoir, filling in any gaps around the edge.

3 When the tank is firmly in place, make sure that it is perfectly level using a level, otherwise the water won't cascade evenly over the pot rim. This reservoir, with its overlapping collar, is known as a Mexican hat.

Setting up a low-maintenance water feature *continued*

4 Put the submersible pump into the tank and position the outlet pipe in the center, ready for the cover to be added. The wide rim ensures that, even when it is windy, water will return to the reservoir.

5 Lift the terra-cotta pot into position. Feed the pump pipe up through the central drainage hole and seal with silicone sealant. You can use a variety of ornamental pots or drilled water sculptures with this type of DIY kit.

6 Attach a long section of delivery piping to the water-flow adjuster. Then attach the delivery pipe and flow adjuster to the pump tube at the base of the pot. The delivery pipe should reach just under the rim of the pot.

7 Fill the reservoir and pot with water. Switch on the pump and test the unit. Too strong a flow and you risk water splashing over the rim. Use the flow adjuster to achieve a gentle flow over the top of the pot.

8 The electrical cord must be protected with a conduit—a qualified electrician will advise you on this and will install an outdoor electricity supply. Ensure that all electrical connections are equipped with a GFCI.

9 Conceal the plastic lid of the reservoir with gravel, leaving a small gap clear for topping off the water. You could also plant the margins with attractive, grassy-leaved plants like evergreen sedges (*Carex*) or *Acorus*.

10 Arrange washed pebbles, cobbles, or rocks of varying sizes around the base of the container to create a naturalistic effect. A small uplighter could be installed to illuminate the feature at night.

Easy lawns and green alternatives

There are several ways to reduce the number of hours spent tending conventional lawns, but if you want to forget about mowing altogether, you could consider replacing a lawn with one of the alternatives shown opposite.

Reducing lawn maintenance To cut down on lawn care, simplify the shape, install a mowing edge, and reduce the area to be mown regularly by replacing with a wildflower meadow (*see p.78*). Also consider easy-care seed mixtures.

This delightful informal area mimics a wildflower meadow and only needs to be cut once or twice a year.

Using suitable lawn-seed mixes You can buy a wide range of grass-seed mixtures for sowing new lawns, as well as for patching worn areas. The best times to sow are mid-spring and mid-fall, but you can sow at any time in between, so long as the soil is warm and moist. There is considerably less choice in sod, although you can usually select between fine lawn or a hardier general-purpose type.

Newly developed mixtures reduce the need for mowing, fertilizing, and irrigation, as they combine naturally short-growing grasses with dwarf clovers called microclovers. The latter have excellent drought resistance coupled with an ability to manufacture their own nitrogen fertilizer, but you won't be able to use lawn weedkiller on them. If you simply want a lawn to create a pleasing foil for borders, then this would be ideal. However, where there is heavy foot traffic and wear and tear from ball games, choose a hard-wearing seed mix containing one of the improved varieties of perennial rye grass. If the lawn is in dappled shade and the sod is thin and colonized with mosses, consider re-sowing with a shady lawn mix.

Lawn alternatives

Succulent carpets Plant drought-tolerant succulents into a sandy soil mix to ensure sharp drainage. Use carpeting sedum species like *Sedum acre*, houseleeks (*Sempervivum*), *Jovibarba* or, in warm sheltered areas, *Echeveria* (*above*).

Shade suitors Plain or variegated *Pachysandra terminalis* (*above*) has glossy evergreen rosettes and makes a good shade-loving alternative to grass. Also consider a dark green ivy (*Hedera helix*), which can be trimmed annually.

Grass lookalikes Some evergreen, grasslike plants, like dwarf sedges (*Carex*) and the two drought-resistant lilyturf (*Ophiopogon*) varieties (*above*), make excellent easy-care replacements for turf, and suit contemporary designs well.

Aromatic footsteps Creeping herbs create lawnlike carpets but, rather than walking on the plants, lay some stepping stones. Try creeping thyme (*above*), pennyroyal, Corsican mint, or the nonflowering chamomile, 'Treneague'.

How to plant

Even low-maintenance gardens can be filled with a beautiful collection of plants. The trick is to select them carefully, matching plants to your site to be sure they will thrive there, and getting them off to a good start by planting with care. This chapter shows you how to test and improve your soil, and includes advice on planting methods for a range of different plants and containers. These techniques will help to increase the health and longevity of your plants, thereby reducing your workload for years to come.

Assessing soil

It is discouraging to see plants struggle because the conditions don't suit them. Knowing what kind of soil you have will help you decide which plants will thrive in your garden, and ensure that you get the very best results.

Different soils

It's the luck of the draw whether your garden has deep, fertile loam or a thin coating of poor, stony topsoil. But whatever your ground is like, it can be improved to expand your planting repertoire and to overcome cultivation problems. To save time and money, however, once you have discovered your soil's strengths and weaknesses, it's best to simply accept its limitations. Don't fight your soil type. If it is lime-rich, showing alkaline in your soil pH test, it won't ever be suitable for ericaceous or lime-hating plants like rhododendrons. If it is acidic, sticky, and water-logged in winter, drought-tolerant herbs and Mediterranean shrubs will rot and die, or sulk miserably.

The clay content of a soil determines its moisture-holding capacity and potential fertility. Clay is ideal for "hungry" plants such as roses. Sand content determines how free-draining your soil will be. The ideal soil, known as loam, is rich in decomposed plant material, making it appear dark, and contains a good mix of both sand and clay particles.

Assessing acidity

Look around the neighbourhood gardens to work out whether your soil is likely to be acidic (lime-free) or alkaline (lime-rich). Healthy-looking ericaceous or lime-hating plants, including camellia, *Pieris*, azalea, and rhododendron, indicate acidic conditions. Soils flecked with white (lumps of limestone) that foster Mediterranean herbs and cornfield annuals are likely to be alkaline. There's only one way to be certain, though, and that's using a soil pH test kit, available from garden centers.

Take samples of soil from a few locations around the garden, mix with the reagent, and compare the color of the liquid with the pH chart; the pH scale runs from 14 (extremely alkaline) to 1 (extremely acidic), with 7 being neutral and close to the gardener's ideal.

Following the instructions on the package, collect a small soil sample and mix it in the tube provided. Wait for the sediment to clear.

Soil must be identified before it can be improved; there are different ways to boost drainage, fertility, or moisture retention.

Eventually, the soil particles settle and the liquid reveals a chemical reaction. Match the color to the card to determine pH.

Testing sandy soil

Soil overlaying sandstones, or close to sandy beaches and dunes, often contains a high proportion of quartz grains. This gives the soil a gritty feel when worked through the fingertips. The more sand a soil contains, the more it will crumble when a handful is compressed, as it has very little of the sticky bonding agent supplied by clay particles.

Sandy soil is easy to dig over and weed—the soil shakes off roots with a few flicks. It also heats up earlier than clays in spring because it is so well drained, but precious nutrients are washed away, too, making it inherently poor. Sandy soil is often, though not always, neutral to acidic in nature. Use a pH kit to find out.

Testing clay soil

Often regarded as a major problem by gardeners, clay soil is potentially the most fertile and productive. If you are lucky, solid clay, which is orange or yellow and sticky, will be covered in a deep layer of darker, more crumbly topsoil.

Sometimes the clay is gray-blue at lower depths, which indicates very poor drainage and ground starved of oxygen. Clay particles are extremely fine and slippery when wet, forming a dense paste that sticks to boots and garden tools. Compacted clay makes an impermeable layer that causes waterlogging, and makes it hard for plant roots and earthworms to push through. When dry, clay sets like concrete and large cracks open up in drought. To test clay content, try the following:

Try rubbing the soil sample through your fingertips. Soil with a high sand content will feel coarse, gritty, and dry.

If you can mold your soil sample in your hands and get it to hold a shape, you have clay. When moistened, it feels slimy.

Squeeze and release a handful of soil, then press lightly with your thumb. Sandy soils crumble under pressure and won't yield moisture.

Try rolling the sample into a sausage. If you can then bend it around into a ring, this indicates a very high clay content.

Improving your soil

Most garden soil benefits from some preparation before planting, as well as ongoing treatments to keep it fertile.

Compacted soil needs digging to increase drainage, and both heavy clay and light sandy soil can be improved.

Increasing drainage in clay soils Don't walk on clay when it is wet and sticky—you will damage the soil structure and worsen the drainage problem. Similarly, it's no use digging rock-hard clay in summer, as the clods break up to dust. However, there are several ways to create the desired free-draining crumb structure.

Digging is an important cultivation method, and you can work the soil earlier in the season if you keep clay dry through winter under a covering of plastic sheeting. Digging in copious quantities of poultry grit improves surface drainage, but if the water table is high, also consider raising the border by adding more soil or banking the soil to make a domed profile.

Incorporating large amounts of coarse organic matter, such as well-rotted manure or spent mushroom compost, into the top layer will also increase drainage. Acidic clay soil can be broken up by applying a top-dressing of garden lime in spring, but don't then use fertilizer as the two do not mix.

Improving fertility and moisture in sandy soil
Well-drained sandy soil can be cultivated year-round, but the depth of fertile topsoil that plants can root into may be quite thin. The underlying subsoil is often compacted and mixed with rock fragments, and is a lighter color by comparison. You should avoid bringing this infertile layer to the surface.

In late winter or early spring, before perennials start into growth, add a layer of well-rotted manure, spent mushroom compost, or garden compost, at least 4 in (10 cm) deep. This functions as a mulch, sealing in the winter moisture and making soils less susceptible to summer drought. It also increases fertility in the soil around the plants' roots. Repeat this process annually for the best results.

Plants for clay soil These are tough and tolerant of soils that may either dry out in summer or become waterlogged in winter. Their roots are often thick and wiry.

- *Amelanchier* 'Ballerina'
- *Berberis thunbergii*
- *Cornus alba*
- *Geranium* x *oxonianum*
- *Hemerocallis*
- *Hydrangea arborescens*
- *Phormium tenax*
- *Physocarpus*
- *Potentilla fruticosa*
- *Rosa*
- *Rudbeckia fulgida*
- *Sambucus*
- *Spiraea* 'Arguta'
- *Viburnum opulus*

Plants for sandy soil Tender plants and those requiring sharp drainage thrive on sand; they include silver-leaved and succulent plants, evergreen shrubs, and perennials.

- *Agapanthus* 'Loch Hope'
- *Ceanothus*
- *Ceratostigma*
- *Convolvulus cneorum*
- *Eryngium*
- *Euphorbia*
- *Hebe*
- *Helictotrichon*
- *Kniphofia*
- *Lavatera* 'Barnsley'
- *Penstemon*
- *Rhodanthemum*
- *Sedum*
- *Yucca*

Weigela   Rosa rugosa   Artemisia ludoviciana   Verbena bonariensis

Plants for acidic soil These are plants of poorly drained heathlands as well as shade-loving woodlanders that enjoy soils rich in decayed leaf litter. Many cannot tolerate lime.

- *Astilbe*
- *Calluna vulgaris*
- *Camellia*
- *Fothergilla major*
- *Gaultheria procumbens*
- *Heuchera*
- *Hydrangea* (blue)
- *Kalmia latifolia*
- *Leucothoe*
- *Pieris*
- *Polystichum setiferum*
- *Rhododendron*
- *Skimmia*
- *Vaccinium*

Plants for alkaline soil Soils over chalk and limestone are alkaline and typically thin and well-drained. Many sun-loving Mediterranean shrubs and herbs are lime-tolerant.

- *Abelia*
- *Buddleja davidii*
- *Buxus sempervirens*
- *Campanula*
- *Cyclamen hederifolium*
- *Dianthus*
- *Escallonia*
- *Iris pallida*
- *Knautia macedonica*
- *Lavandula*
- *Origanum*
- *Pittosporum*
- *Rosmarinus*
- *Sempervivum*

Erica cinerea   Rhododendron   Cistus x dansereaui   Scabiosa columbaria

Clearing your site

Removing weeds, overgrown plants, trees, and debris can be hard work, and you may need to hire expert contractors like arborists. Even in a brand-new garden, rubble could be buried beneath a veneer of topsoil and sod.

First things first Gather as much waste as possible before renting a dumpster, so that you can calculate the correct size and type. Check also whether you need to remove any rotten fencing panels or garden structures. If you plan to remove any big trees, check with your municipality first to check whether you need permission to carry out the work. In new gardens, investigate how much topsoil you have and the condition of the ground below; you may have to dig a series of test pits. Telltale signs of badly drained or compacted subsoil are constantly sodden lawns and pooling water. In dry weather, scorched sod may indicate buried material.

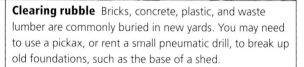

Spraying pernicious weeds Perennial weeds, like ground elder, bindweed, and couch grass, are difficult to eradicate by digging; it is more effective to spray with a systemic weedkiller containing glyphosate, repeating as necessary.

Clearing rubble Bricks, concrete, plastic, and waste lumber are commonly buried in new yards. You may need to use a pickax, or rent a small pneumatic drill, to break up old foundations, such as the base of a shed.

Digging out weeds

You can dig out by hand annual and perennial weeds, bird-sown ornamentals, tree saplings, and brambles. Although this is hard work in clay, in light, sandy ground the soil falls away from the roots easily. When dealing with perennials, try to get all fragments of root out, as any bits left in the ground will almost certainly reshoot. Do not compost.

Dig out perennial weeds like dandelion, buttercup, dock, and thistle, making sure that you lift the whole plant, including the roots.

Fragments like this piece of dandelion taproot are capable of regrowing. With persistence, digging can eliminate problem weeds.

Suppressing weeds with a mulch

This method is ideal for tackling problem weeds in large gardens. Ground elder, couch grass, and mare's-tail require two seasons under cover to guarantee eradication. Use old carpet or underlay to starve plants of light in unused areas. Where beds are infested with weeds, cut them back and lay a landscape membrane over them (*see pp.70–71*).

Cut back weeds to ground level; spraying foliage beforehand with a systemic weed killer is helpful, as the roots start to die off earlier.

Cover weeds with a membrane, so that no light can reach them, and secure the edges. Camouflage with bark chips or aggregates.

Right plant, right place

Whatever the conditions in your garden, keep plants trouble-free by choosing a spot that's just right for them in terms of light, soil type, and moisture.

Check plant labels The information on the label will help you to choose plants that suit your site, so check it carefully. It is often presented as a photograph and series of symbols. These usually state flowering months; height and spread in ten years; moisture levels; sun or shade preferences; and the required acidity or alkalinity of the soil. You may also be warned if the plant is poisonous or an irritant.

Forsythia suspensa needs annual pruning.

High-maintenance pruning Plants in this category include early, large-flowering clematis, mock orange (*Philadelphus*), forsythia, kerria, and weigela. These plants need attention at specific times of year—for example, after flowering—and only certain parts of the plant are pruned. You need to be aware of the difference between younger and older growth, as well as whether particular stems have flowered or are going to provide flowers later on. If you don't feel confident making these observations, then stick to low- or no-prune plants.

Certain plants are also extremely vigorous, and may need to be cut back several times a year to stop them from taking over. Others, like snowberry (*Symphoricarpos*), quickly form spreading thickets. Consider removing nuisance plants.

Low-maintenance pruning Although gardening books often recommend specific pruning regimens, many plants don't need regular attention and thrive when left to their own devices for a few years. These include rambler roses, variegated dogwoods (*Cornus alba* cultivars), and late-flowering clematis.

Most evergreens require very little pruning, other than to control size and trim off frost damage or the odd wayward shoot. Various foliage plants can also be shaped with shears. Mophead and lacecap hydrangeas (*Hydrangea macrophylla*) are easy to maintain—just deadhead them in spring. Shrubs and climbers that are cut back hard in spring—for example, *Buddleja davidii*, clematis (*viticella* forms), shrubby mallow (*Lavatera*), and colored-leaf elders (*Sambucus*)—need no pruning experience.

Hebe 'Red Edge' rarely requires a trim.

Plants for sun It's reasonably easy to spot plants that thrive in sunny, dry places. Some have succulent or thick, fleshy leaves capable of storing water, such as the houseleek (*Sempervivum*). Others, like rosemary, juniper, and blue-leaved grasses, have very small, needlelike leaves with only a tiny surface area from which water can evaporate. Silver or gray plants trap moisture in their felted, furry, or woolly foliage, and do well in full sun and midday heat.

Because many sun-lovers are adapted for drought, they prefer well-drained soils and dislike winter waterlogging. Some slightly tender Mediterranean, Australasian, and South American plants can withstand colder temperatures when kept very dry throughout winter. In clay soil, growing borderline hardy plants, like diascias, in pots is a useful technique.

Sempervivum tectorum | Stachys byzantina

Dryopteris | Hydrangea arborescens

Plants for shade The leaves of shade plants, like hostas, are generally larger than average to absorb maximum light, and plants that thrive in heavy shade have plain green foliage, rather than variegated, red or purple leaves.

Many acid-loving or lime-sensitive shrubs, perennials, and bulbs evolved on the deep, acidic leafmold beneath deciduous trees. Shrubs that thrive in this environment include rhododendron, camellia, skimmia, pieris, and hydrangea. Ferns are classic woodland plants, and most hardy spring-flowering bulbs and perennials, such as snowdrops and hellebores, are shade-tolerant.

Most shade plants dislike drying out in summer, so free-draining soils need to be heavily mulched and improved with well-rotted manure or compost. Many plants, including Japanese maples, also suffer in exposed sites.

Spotting thugs You can often tell when a prospective purchase is likely to get out of hand by looking at the way it is growing in the pot. Herbaceous plants may be climbing over the sides or escaping through the drainage holes. Climbers with widely spaced leaves and long stems reaching far beyond their support canes should be treated with caution. And shrubs whose growth could be described as the opposite of "compact"—long, whippy stems and sparse branching—are destined to cause trouble.

Check the average height and spread figures on the label. Do they seem too high? And look out for telltale phrases like "fast-spreading ground cover." Finally, beware of self-seeders like lady's mantle (*Alchemilla mollis*).

Fallopia baldschuanica | Lysimachia punctata

Different planting techniques

How carefully you select your plants at the garden center or nursery—and how well you nurture them at planting time—makes a considerable difference. The recipe for success in your garden is to start with the very best ingredients.

Choosing healthy plants

Discard any plants with discolored or malformed leaves, as these indicate insect infestation or disease. Forget flowers and look for plants with plentiful leaves, shoots, and new buds. Check that shrubs and trees are well branched and avoid any lopsided specimens or those with a damaged leading shoot. Don't just buy the biggest: smaller, more youthful plants often establish quickly and overtake older ones. When buying grafted plants (you'll see a swelling toward the base of the stem), make sure that the graft union is solid.

Protruding roots A mat of roots through the drainage holes indicates a potbound plant. This can slow the establishment rate after planting.

Weedy pots Avoid weed-choked pots. Weeds weaken a plant and are a sign of general neglect. Remove any surface weeds before planting.

General planting tips

No matter how moist the surface of the soil feels, before planting, submerge each potted specimen in a pail of water until the escaping bubbles dissipate; then remove and drain. Trim back any dead or damaged growth and, after removing the pot, any overly long roots. Dig over the area to be planted, improving the soil as necessary.

Planting levels Dig the planting hole deep enough to accommodate the root ball so that the plant is at the same depth as it was in its pot.

Firming in Check that the plant is level and that you haven't buried any foliage. Firm the soil with your hands (or gently with a foot).

Watering Using a watering can, give the new plant a long drink. This helps to fill soil gaps around the root ball and moistens the surrounding ground.

Planting bulbs

1 It is much easier to dig one large hole, big enough to accommodate several bulbs, than to dig them individually with a trowel or bulb planter. Loosen the soil at the base with a fork to improve drainage and root penetration.

2 Check bulb planting depth and spacing (this is usually stated on the package) and set out the bulbs as shown. Very close planting gives instant impact, but clumps will need to be lifted and divided more frequently.

Bulbs in pots

3 Cover the bulbs with the excavated soil and, if necessary, replace the lawn sod. Especially where squirrels and other digging animals are known to be active, protect bulbs by pegging down sheets of galvanized chicken wire.

Cover the drainage holes with fine mesh and add a layer of gravel and potting mix. Plant the bulbs close together for instant impact—place lily bulbs (*above*) on their sides to prevent them from rotting. Fill the container with potting mix and water well.

Planting herbs through a membrane

Create an easy-care herb garden by planting through a weed-suppressing membrane and finishing it off with a layer of decorative material such as slate or gravel.

Tip for success

Weeds can germinate in tiny traces of soil, so be sure to brush off any crumbs after planting to leave the membrane clean and ready for a topping of gravel.

1 Dig over the soil to ensure that it is soft and easy for new roots to establish, and level the surface—depressions can lead to drainage problems. Roll out the membrane and cut a cross with a utility knife or scissors.

2 Fold back the membrane temporarily to allow for planting. Using a hand trowel, dig out sufficient soil and place in a pail or on a tarp. Place the plant in the prepared hole.

3 Using some of the excavated soil, carefully fill the spaces around the root ball, removing air pockets, and firm in gently with your hands for good root/soil contact. Tuck the membrane flaps back around the neck of the plant.

4 Having cleaned off excess soil, apply a decorative mulch of gravel or slate, lifting up trailing stems or branches to ensure cover right up to the base of the plant. Water well to settle the roots in. Top off the mulch as necessary.

Planting a tree

The best time to establish a deciduous tree is during the dormant season, from early fall to early spring, though pot-grown specimens can be planted year-round.

Tip for success

Insert a piece of perforated drainage tubing into the planting hole close to the roots; leave one end protruding. Watering into the tube directs moisture to where it is most needed.

1 Dig a large hole deep enough to accommodate the root ball. Check with a cane that the top is just at or above ground level. Water the tree, then gently remove the pot—or the wrapping if it is a bare-root tree.

2 Very gently, ease some of the thicker roots from the root ball so that the tips are pointing outward. Tree roots of pot-grown plants often end up tightly coiled and, if left in a tangle, are slow to establish and the tree may die.

3 Ask someone to hold the tree upright, and at the right level, while you start to fill the hole with the excavated soil. Firm in the soil as you backfill, first with your hands and then gently with your feet.

4 Drive a stake in at an angle leaning into the prevailing wind, and fasten to the stem with a tree tie about a third of the way up from the ground. This diagonal stake supports the tree while allowing the stem to strengthen.

Planting a slow-growing hedge

Long-lived, hardy evergreens with dense foliage, like yew, holly, and boxwood, make ideal, easy-care garden hedges. Container-grown plants are available all year, and bare-root or root-balled types are sold in late winter or spring.

Tip for success

After watering the new plants, apply a deep mulch of bark chips or well-rotted manure, leaving gaps around the stems. This will seal in moisture and encourage rooting.

1 Prepare the ground by digging over a strip, 3 ft (1 m) wide, to a spade's depth. Incorporate well-rotted manure or compost to improve soil structure. Stretch a line as a guide and dig a trench that's wide enough for the plants.

2 Make a planting guide by first marking a distance of 20–24 in (50–60 cm) on a piece of wood or cardboard. Then place bamboo canes at these intervals along the string guide, and insert one plant beside each one.

3 Position plants at the same depth as they were originally; on bare-root types, look for the dark stain on the stem. Hold the plant firmly in place while you move the excavated soil back into the trench to support the roots.

4 Continue backfilling the trench and then firm the plants in with your foot, ensuring good contact between soil and roots. Don't press too hard. Roughly level the surface and water thoroughly. Consider irrigating with a soaker hose.

Planting a climbing hydrangea

The soil at the base of a wall or fence can be very dry, but this technique helps to ensure that a climber planted in this position will grow into a strong and healthy specimen.

Tip for success

For self-clingers, like hydrangea, use wall ties that hold the shoots against the wood to encourage the formation of aerial roots. Attach to the fence with a nail and loop around the stem.

1 Improve the moisture-holding capacity and fertility of the soil by digging in well-rotted manure to a spade's depth. To encourage strong root growth beyond the planting hole, dig manure into a square yard (meter) of soil around it.

2 Dig a hole large enough to accommodate the root ball, at least 18 in (45 cm) from the fence. Having presoaked the roots in a pail, plant the hydrangea, angling the stems back toward the fence so that they touch the wood.

3 Backfill with some of the excavated soil-and-manure mix, firming in lightly with your hand. Leave a shallow depression around the base to act as a water reservoir, allowing moisture to collect. Position a fan of canes.

4 Spread the stems out, covering as large an area as possible, and tie to the canes using soft twine. New shoots will fill the gaps. Settle the soil around the roots by watering thoroughly, using a gentle spray to prevent soil erosion.

Creating a meadow effect

With the right preparation, a wildflower meadow can be an easy-care option for your garden; it will reduce the area of mown grass and make decorative use of hard-to-maintain corners. You can even adapt existing lawns.

Caring for your wildflower meadow

For a meadow effect using cornfield annuals (*see right*), sow field poppy, cornflower, corn cockle, corn marigold, and corn chamomile in fall or spring on weed-free soil. Turn the soil each year in spring to cause the fallen seed to germinate, and rake in additional seed to guarantee displays. For a perennial meadow (*see opposite*), cut plants back periodically in the first year to help them establish. Most plants will start flowering from the second year. Bridge the flowering gap with cornfield annuals.

Mowing a path through long grass The pleasing contrast between long and short grass can be formal (*see above*) or informal, with meandering pathways. Areas left to grow and flower may contain a wider variety of species than you expect. Dig out or spot-weed coarse colonizers, like thistle, dock, or tree seedlings, and cut long grass annually in early fall. Plant daffodils to naturalize and buy plug plants—ox-eye daisy and taller biennials, such as teasel and wild carrot—to plant into the tall grass in spring.

Creating a flowering lawn Lawns that haven't been treated regularly with weedkiller and that are relatively poor in nutrients—unfed or on sandy soil—are perfect for turning into a flowery lawn. These lawns will almost certainly already contain a wide range of low-growing wild flowers including hawkbit, white and red clover, daisy, yarrow, plantain, self-heal, bird's-foot trefoil, and speedwell. Infrequent mowing allows the sod to flower in flushes but still be cut again with relative ease.

Sowing a meadow

1 Using seed from a wildflower specialist, spring sow either a mix containing solely perennial wild flowers or one combined with noninvasive grasses. The sowing density instructions should be in the catalog or on the pack.

2 To improve results in fertile clay, or soil badly contaminated with perennial weeds, remove at least a spade's depth of topsoil. Replace with weed-free and poor sandy soil that hasn't been treated with manure.

3 Poorly drained or fertile soils also benefit from a thick top-dressing of sand. Divide the plot roughly into yard or meter squares using canes or twine. To further aid sowing, mix the seed with washed sand and sow evenly in the squares.

4 Firm seed with the back of a rake, bringing it in close contact with the soil. Water thoroughly if it doesn't rain within a few days of sowing. Remove any perennial weeds during early establishment.

Choosing containers

The type of pot you select depends on the style of your garden and your preference for certain materials—each has advantages and disadvantages.

Size matters

The roots of container plants are more, or less, vulnerable to drying out or getting too hot or too cold, depending on the size of the pot, as well as the material it is made from. Vigorous plants in small containers quickly become root-bound and require more frequent watering and fertilizing. Taller specimens may become top-heavy and unstable if the container is too small, or the base isn't wide enough.

Clay Terra-cotta comes in a range of styles including rustic, classical, and contemporary. Unglazed clay can be either very pale with dusty white salts, or a dark orange. Glazed clay, available in many colors, is naturally frost-resistant. Buy guaranteed frostproof pots where possible.

Pros Porous and therefore helping to keep soil drained and aerated, terra-cotta is ideal for growing alpines, succulents, tender perennials, and shrubs that dislike winter rain. The surface weathers and develops an interesting patina over time.

Cons Terra-cotta chips and cracks easily and is susceptible to frost damage, as are any ornate decorations. Empty any pots that are not frostproof and store under cover in fall. Clay is a poor root insulator, so pots may need wrapping if they are left *in situ* during the winter.

Wood A natural material, wood works well in wildlife gardens, cottage-style gardens, and against wood siding and stone buildings. Recycled oak barrels and half-barrels, as well as softwood reproductions, are readily available. Stained or painted planters also suit formal gardens.

Pros Large wooden barrels accommodate the root systems of small trees, tall bamboos, and large evergreen shrubs. Oak is naturally rot-resistant. Thick-sided barrels and planters insulate roots, protecting them from frost.

Cons The metal bands on barrels slip if the wood dries out completely. Wood eventually rots, so planters must be sealed inside (painted with epoxy) or lined with heavy plastic sheeting. Painted or varnished planters need regular retouching.

Synthetic Plastic, resin, or fiberglass materials can now be made into remarkably convincing lightweight replicas of ornate stoneware, terra-cotta, lead, and even Versailles planters. Often, but not always, these reproductions are cheaper than the originals and, once planted, it's almost impossible to tell them apart.

Pros Synthetic containers are extremely light. You can buy giant terra-cotta pots or stonework urns and lift them with ease. There's no need to apply any protective coating, they don't chip, and they are relatively good root insulators.

Cons You may have to make drainage holes in the base and add stones or bricks to weigh pots down. Bright plastic "terra-cotta" might need a coat of acrylic paint to artificially weather the surface, and cheaper plastic pots become brittle and fade in full sun.

Stone Classical designs are perfect for formal or period gardens, but antique carved stone and cast stonework reproductions are expensive. Modern designs in terrazzo, a reconstituted stone with a smooth veneer, are increasingly popular. Alpine enthusiasts can buy rough-hewn troughs.

Pros Stone has a weight and permanence that suits outdoor settings well and, unlike plastic and resin reproductions, pots and planters won't blow over in windy gardens. The thick walls of stone planters insulate roots from cold and keep potting mix moist.

Cons New stonework looks raw at first; try painting it with a commercial aging solution. As stone is very heavy, you should take care when lifting containers and avoid using unstable or top-heavy planters where children play. Reconstituted stone chips to reveal an ugly interior.

Metal Contemporary gardens often feature simple pots made from galvanized zinc and aluminum, or stainless steel; they may be brightly colored or treated to resemble copper, bronze, or rusting iron. Salvaged coppers and antique lead cisterns suit older properties.

Pros Modern metal containers are incredibly lightweight. They come in a range of sculptural shapes, which are not available in other materials, and contemporary color finishes that suit *avant garde* designs. The reflective quality of silvery pots makes them ideal for lightening shady areas.

Cons Some containers don't have drainage holes and need drilling. Watch out for sharp edges when handling. Check surface coatings regularly for rust spots. Insulate containers, as shown, to prevent plant roots from getting too hot in summer and too cold in winter.

Planting a large container

Half-barrels are ideal for permanent plantings, as they allow plenty of room for growth and the wood insulates the roots. Here we've used a mix of evergreen, shade-tolerant perennials, highlighted with annual busy Lizzies.

Tip for success

Sprinkle slow-release fertilizer granules around the plants and lightly work into the soil. These will provide a steady supply of nutrients throughout the growing season.

1   If not already present, drill several drainage holes in the base of the barrel. Cover the base with a piece of fine mesh plastic, or wire netting, to prevent the holes from clogging up with soil and impairing drainage.

2   Pour gravel or stone chips evenly over the mesh to a depth of 2 in (5 cm) or more. This provides a drainage layer that will help prevent the roots from getting too wet, whatever the weather.

3   Half-fill the barrel with a good quality soil-based potting mix. Arrange the plants—hostas, ferns, *Heuchera* 'Pewter Moon', and grassy-leaved *Acorus gramineus* 'Ogon'—until you are happy with the look.

4   Begin planting, allowing 2 in (5 cm) between the rim of the barrel and soil surface for watering. Add the busy Lizzies (bedding *Impatiens*) in any gaps. In fall, these could be replaced with dwarf daffodils. Water thoroughly.

Mulching options

Your choice of mulching materials depends on whether you are looking for an attractive, low-maintenance surface, which can be provided by aggregates or bark, or whether your priority is to fertilize and improve the soil.

Why mulch?

The chief reasons for applying mulches are to suppress weeds and retain moisture. Spread organic mulches—including well-rotted manure, homemade kitchen compost and leafmold, spent mushroom compost, composted seaweed, cocoa shells, and chipped bark—directly onto the soil, leaving gaps around woody stems. They supply valuable plant nutrients and preserve moisture. Bark uses up small amounts of nitrogen during decomposition, so apply after a surface dressing of fertilizer, especially when mulching a newly planted border. Aggregates are usually laid over landscape membrane to prevent weed growth; as a pot mulch, they help prevent soil erosion.

Pebble mulch Rounded pebbles and cobbles contrast beautifully with flat surfaces like paving and gravel. Try grading different sizes of pebbles and add boulders to create naturalistic stream bank or beach effects.

Gravel River stone and water-worn gravel has a more natural look than sharp-edged stone chips. The various grades and colors can be used to mulch around dry garden plants, grasses, and Mediterranean-style plantings.

Bark chips This is an easy-to-apply, weed-free product that comes in different grades. The coarser forms take longer to break down, so they last longer before needing to be topped off, but they are not as ornamental.

Aggregates These include stone chips, slate waste, recycled glass, and acrylic chips. Bright synthetic aggregates make striking low-maintenance surfaces for contemporary gardens and mulches for modern planters.

Homemade compost Compost made from vegetable and fruit scraps, grass clippings, and annual weeds, as well as layers of cardboard and newspaper, is an excellent mulch, which both feeds the soil and locks in moisture.

Cocoa shells Apply this cocoa by-product to a depth of 2 in (5 cm), leaving a small gap around the necks of the plants. Water it thoroughly afterward to bind the mix and create a moisture-retentive crust.

Well-rotted manure and leafmold In early spring, apply well-rotted manure or leafmold, 3 in (8 cm) deep, to enrich the soil and seal in moisture. Make leafmold by packing punctured garbage bags with fall leaves; leave for 2–3 years.

Planting ideas

Whether you favor bright, sunny colors, or muted, subtle shades, creating the perfect planting plan is never easy, even for experienced designers. To make the task easier, the following recipes show exciting planting combinations for different seasons and a range of garden styles. The symbols below are used in each recipe to indicate the conditions the plants prefer.

Key to plant symbols
Soil preference

- ⬤   Well-drained soil
- ◐   Moist soil
- ◯   Wet soil

Preference for sun or shade

- ☀   Full sun
- ☼   Partial or dappled shade
- ☼   Full shade

Hardiness ratings

- ✳✳✳   Fully hardy plants
- ✳✳   Plants that survive outside in mild regions or sheltered sites

Spring mix

This woodland carpet could be recreated under the dappled shade of deciduous trees or large shrubs. The planting reaches its peak in early spring when the snowdrops open and the bronze-pink fronds of the maidenhair fern (*Adiantum*) unfurl. The marbled arum foliage makes a lovely foil for various forms of hellebore that flower through winter; select these in bloom, as catalog descriptions can be misleading. The colored petals are long-lasting and the nodding flowers of the *H. orientalis* subsp. *guttatus* have speckled throats.

Border basics

Size 5 x 5 ft (1.5 x 1.5 m)
Suits Shade-loving woodland plants that flower in late winter or early spring
Soil Moist, with a deep organic mulch
Site Under trees or north-facing border

Shopping list

- 7 x *Adiantum venustum*
- 9 x *Arum italicum* subsp. *italicum* 'Marmoratum'
- 5 x *Helleborus* x *hybridus* cultivar
- 5 x *Helleborus orientalis* subsp. *guttatus*
- 50–100 x *Galanthus nivalis*

Planting and aftercare

Work in plenty of well-rotted manure, garden compost, or leafmold to improve clay soil or make sandy or free-draining ground more moisture-retentive. Plant the border in fall or in mild spells during winter and early spring. Pot-grown snowdrops, or those lifted and replanted in clumps just after flowering, often establish better than dry bulbs planted in early fall. Mulch with chipped bark or cocoa shells to retain moisture and suppress weeds. Remove old leaves from the hellebores when the flowers start to open so that they don't mar the display. Also snip off dead or damaged leaves from the maidenhair fern when the new fronds unfurl.

Arum italicum subsp. *italicum* 'Marmoratum' ❄❄❄ ◖ ☀

Helleborus orientalis subsp. *guttatus* ❄❄❄ ◖ ☀

Galanthus nivalis ❄❄❄ ◖◖ ☀

Helleborus x *hybridus* cultivar ❄❄❄ ◖ ☀

Adiantum venustum ❄❄❄ ◖ ☀

Sparkling summer bed

This silver and pink color scheme is perfect for a sunny hot spot. Dotted through the planting, metallic-leaved astelia, commonly called silver spear, adds a distinctly Mediterranean feel. The compact form of the evergreen *Artemisia schmidtiana* appears like a shimmering river running through the border, with blue-leaved fescues on one side and pink-flowered thrift or sea pink on the other. The thrift (*Armeria*) blooms from late spring into early summer from wiry green tussocks. At the rear, the cut-leaved artemisia adds height and texture.

Border basics

Size 6 x 5 ft (1.8 x 1.5 m)
Suits Drought-tolerant grasses, alpines, and perennials
Soil Sharply drained
Site Hot, sunny, and sheltered

Shopping list

- 3 x *Astelia chathamica*
- 3 x *Artemisia ludoviciana* 'Valerie Finnis'
- 7 x *Artemisia schmidtiana* 'Nana'
- 7 x *Festuca glauca* 'Blauglut'
- 9 x *Armeria maritima* 'Splendens'

Planting and aftercare

Prepare heavier ground by digging in plenty of grit to improve drainage. This layout is best planted in late spring when the weather has become warmer and drier. Plants like the slightly tender astelia will have a chance to establish before winter and the grasses and silvery artemisias should be in active growth. To maintain the display, cut back dead heads on the thrift and, at the end of the season, the dead stems of the broad-leaved artemisia. Wrap the astelia with horticultural fleece if a cold snap is forecast, and mulch with bark to protect the roots. In spring, tidy the grasses by combing the dead leaves out of the tussocks with your fingers. Lightly trim the evergreen artemisia with shears.

Astelia chathamica
✳✳ ◊ ☼

Artemisia ludoviciana 'Valerie Finnis'
✳✳✳ ◊ ☼

Artemisia schmidtiana 'Nana'
✳✳✳ ◊ ☼

Armeria maritima 'Splendens'
✳✳✳ ◊ ☼

Festuca glauca 'Blauglut'
✳✳✳ ◊ ☼

Elegant fall border

This sparkling arrangement starts blooming in midsummer. First in flower is the pearly everlasting (*Anaphalis*) with clusters of papery ball-shaped heads, which remain attractive for many weeks, over gray-green felted leaves. Mingled in, the vibrant aster 'Veilchenkönigin' is a Michaelmas daisy with compact growth and good disease resistance. At the back, Russian sage (*Perovskia*) makes a delicate but long-lasting foil (try globe thistle, *Echinops*, as an alternative) and clumps of stipa add structure and movement.

Border basics

Size 6 x 4 ft (1.8 x 1.4 m)
Suits Late summer- and fall-flowering perennials and grasses
Soil Well-drained, neutral to alkaline
Site Open, full sun

Shopping list

- 3 x *Stipa calamagrostis*
- 5 x *Aster amellus* 'Veilchenkönigin' syn. Violet Queen
- 5 x *Perovskia atriplicifolia* 'Blue Spire' or 5 x *Echinops ritro*
- 7 x *Anaphalis triplinervis*

Planting and aftercare

The plants in this plan enjoy fertile, well-drained soil, so remedy any drainage problems before planting in spring, and dig in organic matter if the soil is poor and dry. After soaking the pots, lay the plants out in long overlapping drifts. This arrangement suits relatively narrow borders because it creates the illusion of depth. Intermingle the asters and pearl everlasting where the two drifts meet to give a more naturalistic feel. Mulch to retain moisture, keep down weeds, and help plants establish through the summer months. In midwinter, cut down old flower stems of foreground plantings if they look untidy, but delay cutting back the grass and Russian sage until spring.

Stipa calamagrostis
❄❄❄ ◊ ☼

Aster amellus 'Veilchenkönigin'
❄❄❄ ◊ ☼

ovskia atriplicifolia 'Blue Spire'
❋❋ ◊ ☼

Anaphalis triplinervis
❋❋❋ ◊ ☼ ☀

Alternative plant idea

Echinops ritro
❋❋❋ ◊ ☼

Winter color

The flame-colored willow (*Salix*) sets this sunny border alight. It thrives in heavy soil, including waterlogged clay. Hard pruning in spring helps control its vigor, but in a small garden, consider using the dogwood *Cornus sanguinea* 'Midwinter Fire' instead. The ghostly white-stemmed rubus has dainty divided leaves in summer—a subtle contrast with the diaphanous stipa. In heavier soil, consider replacing this grass with the coppery pheasant's tail (*Anemanthele lessoniana*). In winter, the tawny red sedum flowers dry out, forming stiff, long-lasting maroon heads.

Border basics

Size 6 x 6 ft (1.8 x 1.8 m)
Suits Deciduous shrubs, grasses, and late-flowering perennials
Soil Fertile, well-drained, not too dry
Site Full sun

Shopping list

- 1 x *Salix alba* var. *vitellina* 'Britzensis'
- 1 x *Rubus thibetanus*
- 7 x *Sedum* 'Herbstfreude'
- 9–11 x *Stipa tenuissima*

Planting and aftercare

For best results, plant in spring to allow plants to establish before putting on a show through the winter. Cut the white-stemmed rubus and willow back hard the following spring to encourage plenty of new stems, which color up better than the old. Also cut back the grass foliage as you see new growth appearing, and clear away old sedum stems. Every three years lift, and split the sedum clumps in spring to keep them strong and stop them from collapsing during late summer. Apply a granular, slow-release fertilizer annually in spring and/or well-rotted manure at pruning time. Consider adding tall *Verbena bonariensis* for extra color in the "quiet" summer phase of this display.

Salix alba var. *vitellina* 'Britzensis'
❄❄❄ ◐ ◐ ☼

Rubus thibetanus
❄❄❄ ◐ ☼

Sedum 'Herbstfreude'
❄❄❄ ◌ ◐ ☼

Stipa tenuissima
❄❄❄ ◌ ☼

Cool foliage collection

In spring, the lungwort (*Pulmonaria*) puts on a display of white blooms, and the silver-spotted leaves that follow are just as attractive. The cream-variegated elder (*Sambucus*) brightens this shady spot, and clumps of dwarf boxwood (*Buxus*), along with the cherry-red stems of variegated dogwood (*Cornus*), maintain structure in winter. Tall flag iris makes a bold vertical statement and, though normally grown in water, its vigor is controlled in drier soil. Silver curry plants (*Helichrysum*) thrive in a patch of sunlight.

Border basics

Size 6 x 12 ft (1.8 x 4 m)
Suits Shade-tolerant shrubs and perennials grown for foliage contrast
Soil Fertile, moisture-retentive
Site Cool, lightly shaded

Shopping list

- 1 x *Cornus alba* 'Elegantissima'
- 1 x *Sambucus nigra* 'Marginata'
- 3 x *Helichrysum italicum*
- 3 x *Iris pseudacorus* var. *bastardii*
- 7 x *Pulmonaria saccharata* 'Sissinghurst White'
- 3 x *Buxus sempervirens* 'Suffruticosa'

Planting and aftercare

Most plants here would thrive in clay-rich soil. Improve dry soil by working in plenty of well-rotted manure. The curry plant requires sharply drained ground, so dig in plenty of grit before planting, or swap for pearl everlasting (*Anaphalis triplinervis*) as this tolerates clay and shade. Siberian iris (*Iris sibirica*) could also replace the flag iris. Mulch with bark after planting. Clip the boxwood to shape in early summer. In early spring, prune the elder back to a low framework and, once established, remove a third of the oldest stems of the dogwood. Prune the curry plant in spring to keep it bushy, and if mildew attacks the pulmonaria, cut back, fertilize, and water to aid regrowth.

Cornus alba 'Elegantissima'
❋❋❋ ◦ ☼ ◐

Sambucus nigra 'Marginata'
❋❋❋ ◦ ☼ ◐

Helichrysum italicum
❋❋❋ ◦ ☼

Iris pseudacorus var. *bastardii*
❋❋❋ ◦ ◦ ☼ ◐

Pulmonaria saccharata 'Sissinghurst White' ❋❋❋ ◦ ◐ ☼

Buxus sempervirens 'Suffruticosa'
❋❋❋ ◦ ◦ ◐

Architectural designs

All these plants have such a sculptural profile that the overall effect is very dramatic. The yellow-stemmed bamboo (*Phyllostachys*) makes an effective screen and, building a subtropical theme, two bold variegated yuccas dominate the foreground. Giant feather grass (*Stipa gigantea*) carries shimmering seedheads well into fall, its vertical form contrasting with the spreading tussocks of the New Zealand sedge (*Carex comans*). This bronze evergreen's color and form work beautifully with the broad, thick, textured foliage of the blue-leaved hosta and spiky black ophiopogon.

Border basics

Size 8 x 8 ft (2.5 x 2.5 m)
Suits Sculptural evergreens, bamboos, and grasslike plants
Soil Well-drained to moisture-retentive
Site Sunny

Shopping list

- 1 x *Stipa gigantea*
- 1 x *Phyllostachys aureosulcata*
  f. *aureocaulis*
- 2 x *Yucca filamentosa* 'Bright Edge'
- 3 x *Hosta sieboldiana* var. *elegans*
- 5 x *Ophiopogon planiscapus*
  'Nigrescens'
- 3 x *Carex comans* bronze-leaved

Planting and aftercare

Prepare individual planting holes. The stipa, yucca, and ophiopogon thrive in sharply drained soil, so in heavier soil, work in plenty of grit. The sedges, hostas, and bamboo, meanwhile, enjoy moisture-retentive conditions. Improve dry, sandy ground by digging in well-rotted manure. Mulch with bark. The hosta has good slug resistance but watch for damage to new leaves. In spring, cut the sedge back hard, as the regrowth is more colorful, and trim back the old flower stems of the stipa. Cut a few older bamboo canes at the base to maintain an open habit.

Stipa gigantea
❀❀❀ ◊ ☼

Phyllostachys aureosulcata
f. *aureocaulis* ❀❀❀ ◖ ☼ ☼

Yucca filamentosa 'Bright Edge'
❀❀❀ ◊ ☼

Hosta sieboldiana var. elegans
❀❀❀ ◖ ☼

Ophiopogon planiscapus 'Nigrescens'
❀❀❀ ◊ ☼ ☼

Carex comans bronze-leaved
❀❀❀ ◖ ☼ ☼

Easy perennials

With the right plants, you can sit back and enjoy fabulous flowering displays all summer long for next to no effort. This recipe combines colorful blooms and handsome foliage set off against the dark backdrop of a yew hedge. Relatively new on the scene, the blue geranium 'Nimbus' blooms from late spring to midsummer and is furnished with intricately cut foliage. Pincushion-flowered knautia takes over from mid- to late summer accompanied by tall spikes of the ornamental sage 'Ostfriesland'. The silvery felted lamb's ears (*Stachys*) and hairlike stipa make a textural foil.

Border basics

Size 5 x 6 ft (1.5 x 1.8 m)
Suits Easy-care perennials and grasses
Soil Fertile, moist but well-drained
Site Sunny

Shopping list

- 3 x *Geranium* 'Nimbus'
- 5 x *Knautia macedonica*
- 5 x *Salvia nemorosa* 'Ostfriesland'
- 3 x *Stachys byzantina* 'Silver Carpet'
- 5 x *Stipa tenuissima*
- *Taxus baccata* (hedge)

Planting and aftercare

Cut the yew hedge toward the end of summer; leave a gap between the hedge and the border for access. Improve poor, dry soil with well-rotted manure, garden compost, or spent mushroom compost. This arrangement is best planted in spring or early fall. Mulch with bark to control weeds. The following spring, cut plants back to new growth arising from the base—none of them should require staking, but pushing a few twiggy sticks in around the geranium in spring will help stop plants from sprawling too far. Deadhead the knautia as often as you can to prolong flowering. Cutting back geranium foliage after flowering encourages compact, new leafy growth.

Geranium 'Nimbus'
❄❄❄ ○ ◑ ☼ ◑

Knautia macedonica
❄❄❄ ○ ☼

Salvia nemorosa 'Ostfriesland'
❄❄❄ ○ ☼

Stachys byzantina 'Silver Carpet'
❄❄❄ ○ ☼

Stipa tenuissima
❄❄❄ ○ ☼

Taxus baccata
❄❄❄ ○ ☼ ☀

Contemporary prairie

This example of new wave or prairie-style planting is stylish and easy to care for. The ornamental sage, yellow foxglove, and verbena attract bees and butterflies, and if you leave this "meadow" to die down naturally, it will provide a valuable habitat for beneficial insects, small mammals, and birds. Flowering begins with the foxglove (*Digitalis*) and the violet-purple sage ('Mainacht' or 'May Night') in early summer, and reaches a peak in midsummer when the verbena joins the display. Giant feather grass (*Stipa*) throws up tall wands of glistening seedheads which, along with the verbena, last well into fall. You could consider maiden grass (*Miscanthus sinensis* 'Gracillimus') as a tall, narrow-leaved alternative to the stipa.

Border basics

Size 8 x 8 ft (2.5 x 2.5 m)
Suits Grasses, natural-looking perennials
Soil Fertile, well-drained but not dry
Site Sunny, open

Shopping list

- 5 x *Stipa gigantea* or *Miscanthus sinensis* 'Gracillimus'
- 9 x *Verbena bonariensis*
- 7 x *Salvia* x *sylvestris* 'Mainacht'
- 7 x *Digitalis lutea*

Planting and aftercare

Plant in early fall or mid- to late spring, improving dry or poor soil by adding well-rotted manure or garden compost. Lay out the plants in large overlapping blocks or swaths and use the tall, "see-through" verbena at intervals between shorter plants to create a more dynamic and naturalistic arrangement. All of the plants can be left to die down naturally at the end of the season, as the old flower stems and seedheads remain attractive well into the winter. Trim back in spring but leave the evergreen grass tussocks.

Stipa gigantea
❋❋❋ ◊ ☼

Verbena bonariensis
❋❋ ◊ ☼

Salvia x *sylvestris* 'Mainacht'
❋❋❋ ◊ ☼

Digitalis lutea
❋❋❋ ◊ ◑ ☼ ☼

Alternative plant idea

Miscanthus sinensis 'Gracillimus'
❋❋❋ ◑ ☼ ☼

Aromatic herb border

Many traditional herb-garden plants have potential for use in low-maintenance plans, as they are mostly evergreen and drought-resistant. Here, aromatic lavender and common thyme blend with a cream-flowered cotton lavender (*Santolina*) and giant, silver-leaved cardoon (*Cynara*). Wispy bronze sedges weave through the planting, linking the various elements. The resulting slate-mulched bed has a muted, contemporary feel and would work well in full sun, adjacent to an open expanse of paving or decking. Add cream *Crocus chrysanthus* at the front for spring color.

Border basics

Size 6 x 5 ft (1.8 x 1.5 m)
Suits Drought-tolerant herbs, perennials, and sedges
Soil Reasonably fertile, sharply drained
Site Sunny, sheltered from wind

Shopping list

- 3 x *Santolina pinnata* subsp. *neapolitana* 'Edward Bowles'
- 5 x *Thymus vulgaris*
- 1 x *Cynara cardunculus*
- 5 x *Lavandula* 'Fathead'
- 7 x *Carex flagellifera*

Planting and aftercare

Plant between spring and early summer, to give the herbs a chance to establish before winter. Improve the drainage of clay soils by digging in grit or gravel. Soak plants, remove pots, and set out to make a pleasing arrangement. For weed-free gardening, plant through membrane and mulch with slate chips or gravel. Clip over the lavender after flowering in late summer and, in fall, tidy the faded leaves and woody flower stalk of the cardoon. The following spring, cut the cotton lavender back to a low framework, and lightly trim the thymes. Trimming the sedges close to the base in spring encourages colorful regrowth.

Santolina pinnata subsp. *neapolitana* 'Edward Bowles' ❋❋❋ ◊ ☼

Thymus vulgaris ❋❋❋ ◊ ☼

nara cardunculus
❀❀ ◊ ☼

Lavandula 'Fathead'
❀❀❀ ◊ ☼

Carex flagellifera
❀❀❀ ◊ ◑ ☼ ◔

Chic foliage collection

The key to creating a contemporary look is to limit your plan to a single subject or just a handful of texturally interesting plants. Here the pink-leaved phormium adds height and vibrancy, its straplike foliage contrasting strongly with the bold, rounded leaves of the *Bergenia*. Flowering in spring, *Bergenia* 'Red Beauty' gives early-season interest and is followed by the simple white blooms of the convolvulus. An evergreen with leaves like strips of metal, the elegant convolvulus mirrors the silver container and complements the other plants, especially the "black" ophiopogon.

Container basics

Size Galvanized metal container, approx. 16 in (40 cm) in diameter
Suits Architectural evergreen shrubs and perennials
Soil Loam-based, free-draining potting mix
Site Sunny, sheltered from hard frosts

Shopping list

- 1 x *Bergenia* 'Red Beauty'
- 1 x *Ophiopogon planiscapus* 'Nigrescens'
- 1 x *Convolvulus cneorum*
- 1 x *Phormium* 'Jester'

Planting and aftercare

Metal containers heat and cool rapidly, potentially damaging roots, so insulate with a layer of bubble wrap or use a plastic pot as a liner, filling the gap with horticultural fleece. Cover the drainage holes with crocks and pour in 2 in (5 cm) of gravel. Half-fill with a good quality soil-based potting mix, adding slow-release fertilizer at the recommended rate. Arrange the plants to find the best fit, then plunge each pot into a pail of water, drain, and plant. Fill any gaps with more soil and water thoroughly. Water regularly, remove faded bergenia flowers, and renew fertilizer granules annually.

Bergenia 'Red Beauty'
❁❁❁ ◐ ◑ ☀ ◐

Convolvulus cneorum
❁❁ ◐ ☼

Ophiopogon planiscapus 'Nigrescens'
❁❁❁ ◐ ◑ ☼ ◐

Phormium 'Jester'
❁❁ ◐ ☼

Cottage garden in a container

Plain or decorated, terra-cotta tends to fit in well with older historic properties and traditional types of gardens, such as formal or cottage style. When buying, check that the pots are guaranteed frostproof and have no visible cracks or chips; a bell-like ring when struck indicates that the pot is sound. Being porous, clay is ideal for herbs, alpines, succulents, and drought-tolerant plants; if you want to use other plants, and still cut down on watering, it is best to line the pots with plastic.

Diascia 'Sunchimes Lilac'

Lavandula angustifolia 'Hidcote'

Container basics

Size Terra-cotta pot, approx. 15 in (38 cm) in diameter
Suits Mediterranean-style perennials, herbs, and succulents
Soil Loam-based, free-draining potting mix
Site Sunny for most of the day

Shopping list

- 1 x *Lavandula angustifolia* 'Hidcote'
- 2 x *Scabiosa* 'Pink Mist' or *Osteospermum* 'White Pim'
- 1 x *Sedum* 'Ruby Glow'
- 2 x *Diascia* 'Sunchimes Lilac'

Planting and aftercare

Soak the pot until the sides have turned a darker shade, indicating saturation, as this reduces the amount of moisture absorbed from the soil by the clay. Otherwise, line with black plastic, making sure that the drainage holes are uncovered. Protect the holes with fine mesh, flat stones or broken crocks, and add a layer of gravel for drainage. Half fill with loam-based mix combined with a slow-release fertilizer. After soaking the plants, arrange them to create a pleasing display. Carefully fill around the root balls, and finish at a final soil level 2 in (5 cm) below the rim to allow for watering. Regularly deadhead the scabious and diascia, and shear the lavender after flowering.

Scabiosa 'Pink Mist'

Alternative plant idea

Sedum 'Ruby Glow'

Osteospermum 'White Pim'

Caring for your garden

Creating a garden that is low-maintenance does not mean it needs no maintenance, and the advice in this chapter outlines the basic care your garden will require to keep it looking good throughout the year. Tasks such as watering, weeding, and fertilizing should not take too much time, but nevertheless need to be addressed, while dealing promptly with pests and diseases will minimize any damage to your plants. Finally, keep the garden neat with periodic cleaning and pruning.

Watering techniques

During the heat of summer, watering may become a real chore unless you are organized and target only the areas needing attention.

Saving water Apart from the environmental benefits of not wasting tap water on the garden, saving rainwater and recycling "gray" water from the house works both practically and financially. Rainwater is free, and rain barrels positioned at downspouts provide a convenient source for plants; even narrow spots next to sheds can be utilized using slim-line barrels. Install as many barrels as possible to save water in case of a drought.

What to water You should only need to water newly planted specimens, container plants, and freshly laid sod (established lawns never need watering). Planting hardy plants between mid-fall and mid-spring reduces the amount of watering needed during the critical period when roots are establishing; unless there's a drought, these new additions won't need summer watering, especially if given a moisture-conserving mulch, although thirsty ornamentals may need extra water.

Flowering evergreen wall shrubs like camellias, as well as wall-trained fruit trees or berrying plants, are vulnerable to water shortages—even between fall and spring—since the soil is much drier at the foot of a wall. Mulch heavily, and check year-round to ensure that there is sufficient moisture to support buds and fruits.

Watering efficiently Avoid watering in the heat of the day, as moisture evaporates rapidly. Target the roots directly and don't use sprinklers—if you water foliage from above, much of it evaporates or is deflected—but don't blast the ground with a strong jet, as this will erode the soil and expose roots. A gentle flow or trickle allows water time to soak in, rather than just running over the surface. Make shallow depressions with a raised edge around new plants to create a water reservoir directly above their roots. If you water for long enough in one place, moisture penetrates deep into the soil and plant roots grow down in search of it. If you water lightly, and dampen only the top layer of soil, the roots will come up to the surface where they are vulnerable to drought.

Soaker hoses Sometimes called a drip hose or trickle irrigation, this consists of a pipe perforated with numerous small holes. The pipe is laid directly on the soil surface, weaving between plants and, if necessary, is held in place with wire clips. Attached to an outside faucet with leak-proof connectors, the pipe's gentle watering action allows moisture to penetrate deep into the soil.

Soaker hoses are the next best thing to an automatic irrigation system because they allow many plants to be watered at once. They are also ideal for helping new hedges to establish, the water running evenly along the length of the hedge, encouraging strong root establishment. Make sure you clean the hose periodically to keep the perforations clear.

Watering containers As pots are watered frequently, the potting mix quickly erodes to expose roots, especially in the case of shallow-rooting species, like boxwood. Try watering onto a piece of clay pot, to help dissipate the flow, or use a surface mulch of bark, compost, or decorative aggregate.

Don't overfill containers with potting mix—you need a gap of about 2 in (5 cm) between the soil surface and rim to allow water to pool and sink in. Similarly, a slow, gentle water flow is preferable to a strong blast. Devices available from garden centers allow hanging baskets to be lowered and raised for convenient watering, and grouping containers is also more practical than dotting them around the garden.

Nozzles and wands Watering with a hose is much easier and less wasteful when you use a nozzle with an on/off finger trigger, as you don't have to keep going back to the faucet. Choose a nozzle with a broad head and a flow rate that can be adjusted from a strong jet to a gentle shower, the latter setting being much less likely to cause soil erosion.

Nozzles make the daily task of watering numerous patio pots less arduous, and an extended wand attachment (*see right*) gives you a much longer reach—you can get to the back of a group of pots, or up into overhead planters or hanging baskets, much more easily than struggling with a heavy watering can.

Installing automatic irrigation

Pots need a lot of attention during the growing season and some form of automatic watering is a boon when time is limited. Potentially the most efficient in terms of water conservation, irrigation systems can also be adapted for borders.

1 You can buy irrigation systems from larger garden centers, and most include all you need for a small patio; extension pieces are available as required. Each manufacturer's system may use slightly different connection techniques.

2 Check that the containers are in their final positions and measure the distance between the farthest pot and your faucet. Then cut the main tubing to this length, ready to connect the feeder tubes that will supply each pot.

3 Measure the length between the pots and the main tube. Cut the required number of feeder tubes and soak their ends in hot water to soften the plastic. This makes it easier to push them onto the connecting pieces and droppers.

4 Cut the main pipe at each container; soak the ends in hot water. Then push the two sections of main tubing and a feeder tube on to a connecting piece. Attach a drip nozzle to the end of the feeder tube. Repeat for each pot.

5 Connect the automatic timer to an outdoor faucet with a screw thread, and then attach the main pipe. Temporarily override the timer, turn on the water, and check the system for any leaks or blockages.

6 Set the timer to come on as needed—for example, at night or first thing in the morning—for the required number of minutes. Monitor initially to check that you are not over- or underwatering the containers.

7 Some drip nozzles are designed to be inserted along the feeder tubes so that they can water more than one pot. Place each nozzle near the base of the plant to avoid water wastage and hold in place with the supplied pegs.

Feeding your plants

For the best results, plants need a good balance of nutrients throughout the growing season. A range of specialized fertilizers makes such feeding easy.

Signs of nutrient deficiency General fertilizers contain nitrogen (N) for leaf and shoot growth, potassium (K) for flowers and fruits, and phosphorus (P) for healthy roots. Plants deprived of these, and other trace elements, show various symptoms. Small, yellowing leaves and slow growth suggest lack of nitrogen. Sparse blooms and poor fruits may indicate potassium deficiency, but combined with lush, leafy growth means nitrogen overdosing. Dark green leaf veins, surrounded by pale tissue, points to either iron or magnesium deficiency, depending on conditions.

Types of fertilizer

Most ornamental plants do well if given a fertilizer that provides the three vital nutrients—nitrogen, phosphorus and potassium (potash)—as well as trace minerals, through the growing season. But there are many products that cater to the needs of specific plants—for example, roses. Lawn fertilizers have ample nitrogen for healthy-looking sod, while tomato fertilizer is rich in potassium and magnesium for large crops. Mixtures targeting container plants and flower borders have plenty of potassium, and also a good balance of other nutrients to foster shoot and root development.

Bush roses and summer-flowering bedding need a fertilizer containing plenty of potassium and some trace elements to keep them blooming.

Foliage plants, like this hosta, as well as grasses and bamboos, thrive on nitrogen-rich fertilizer and need relatively little potassium.

When and how to apply plant food

In early spring, spread bulky organic material around your plants, leaving a gap around the base of woody species and evergreens.

Top off organic mulches Products like homemade compost, manure, composted seaweed, or spent mushroom compost are rich in minerals and natural fertilizers, as well as biologically active substances that help condition soil and maintain its fertility.

Manure should always be well-rotted (3–4 years old) and from a covered heap so that precious nutrients haven't been washed away by rain. Mushroom compost, available from topsoil suppliers, contains lime and is not suitable for ericaceous or acid-loving plants. While synthetic, slow-release fertilizers are a handy way of keeping plants well fed, it's important, especially on thin sandy soil or heavy clay, to add bulky organic matter too. Applied as a thick mulch in late winter or early spring, it can be worked around emerging herbaceous plants, shrubs, trees, and climbers, to seal in winter moisture and release nutrients into the root zone.

If making your own compost, you can use annual weeds unless they have developed seedheads, but never compost perennial weeds. Animal manure may contain weed seeds and perennial weed roots, but compost produced commercially tends to be sterilized and weed-free.

Slow-release granules For container plants to have all the nutrients they need to grow and flower well, they only need one or two applications of slow-release granules each year. These can be incorporated into the potting mix at planting time, or worked into the surface around plants.

Annual fertilizers Slow-release fertilizers are applied annually in mid-spring to border plants that are starting into growth. They release nutrients according to temperature and moisture levels, and last longer than quick-acting fertilizers. Follow the instructions carefully.

Weeds and common problems

Despite your best efforts to suppress any weeds, some are bound to pop up now and again, so here are a few tips on how best to deal with them. Also included is useful advice on rectifying the most common plant problems and disorders.

Annual weeds Every time you disturb the soil, you bring to the surface hundreds of dormant seeds that will germinate given sufficient light and moisture. Pull out seedlings by hand—or hoe—before they flower, or apply a weed-suppressing mulch to prevent the problem.

Perennial weeds These are not easy to pull out by hand and don't respond to hoeing, since each piece left in the ground can regenerate. Plants like the dandelion (*above*) also set large quantities of seed. Dig out completely, or use a systemic weedkiller, and remove flowerheads promptly.

Self-seeding ornamentals Some flowers, like *Verbena bonariensis* and *Lychnis coronaria*, seed usefully, replacing old plants or those that don't survive the winter. But plants like *Alchemilla mollis* (*above*) are just too successful. Either remove or cut back immediately after flowering.

Problem weeds Plants such as bindweed (*above*), ground elder, and couch grass may reappear even after several doses of systemic weedkiller. Keep a ready-mixed spray for spot treatments and check that mulch is intact. Treat woody subjects like brambles with a brushwood killer.

How to weed

Weeding success is all about timing. If you miss your window of opportunity, and don't get on top of things in spring when weeds are young and easier to remove, the rest of the year can be a struggle without the help of chemicals and mulches. The less you disturb the soil, the fewer weeds appear, so keep digging to a minimum.

Even when gravel is laid on a membrane, weeds still pop up. Remove as seedlings.

Hoe only on dry, sunny days, severing the roots of annual weeds at ground level.

Keep a bottle of ready-mixed systemic weed-killer handy for spot-treating problem weeds.

Dealing with plant disorders

There are a number of reasons, other than attacks by pests or diseases, why certain plants can look unhealthy. They may be planted in the wrong spot and suffer because they are too hot or too shaded, too wet or too dry. Or they may be in a frost pocket, an exposed or windswept corner, or even in the wrong type of soil.

Nutrient deficiency Telltale signs like yellowing leaves, dark veins, slow growth, and poor flowering or fruiting may indicate lack of nutrients. See causes and treatments (*pp.116–117*).

Frost damage Common on evergreen shrubs starting into growth early, like pieris (*above*), or those pruned too late, which then produce sappy growth that isn't frostproof.

Dead wood Parts of a plant may die due to physical damage caused by wind fractures, root problems, or pests and diseases. Remove damaged wood promptly; cut back to healthy stems.

Dealing with pests and diseases

Attacks on plants may take care of themselves without intervention. But it's best to anticipate problems and deal with pests and diseases in the early stages.

Friendly predators Gardens with a healthy balance of pests and predators—the latter including ground beetles, ladybugs, lacewings, hoverflies, as well as insect-eating birds—suffer fewer major infestations. Set aside areas for friendly bugs to breed, shelter, and hibernate, and provide nectar-rich flowers to support hoverfly adults. Resist spraying routinely against pests, as this can also poison predators and starve them of food. Hang feeders and nest boxes to attract birds. A pool will foster slug-eating amphibians.

Ladybugs Adults and larvae are carnivorous, but numbers don't build up until the aphid population is big enough, so avoid reaching for pesticides prematurely. Adults overwinter in sheltered places.

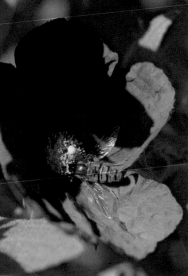

Hoverflies There are many species of these bee- and wasp-mimicking flies; the larvae of some are voracious aphid-eaters. Provide nectar-rich flowers from spring to fall to attract hoverflies into the garden.

Common pests

Slugs and snails These are active at night, so flashlight forays catch culprits in action. Protect vulnerable plantings with dry, gritty mulches. Use biological control nematodes against slugs, or apply pellets sparingly.

Aphids These cause leaf distortions and can spread viruses. Look out for their white skeletons. Check new shoots and flower buds, and rub off or blast with a hose to reduce numbers. Use pesticides sparingly.

Vine weevils The larvae (*inset*) feed on roots and can cause plants to wilt and die. The dull black adults nibble leaf margins. Water with pathogenic nematodes (biological control) or use a vine weevil pesticide.

Common diseases

Powdery mildew This fungus tends to occur in dry spells, so mulch border perennials and water summer containers regularly. Pick off affected shoots or cut plants back hard; fertilize and water to encourage regrowth.

Sooty mold This nonparasitic fungus grows on the honeydew excreted by sap-sucking insects, such as aphids, whiteflies, mealybugs, and scale insects. Wipe off the mold and treat plants with a systemic insecticide.

Rust Different forms attack a range of plants, including hollyhocks and bush roses. Orange pustules on the undersides of leaves carry spores. Avoid overhead watering; remove and destroy infected material in fall.

Botrytis Also called gray mold, this furry fungus is problematic in spring and fall when light levels and temperatures are low and humidity is high. Pick off dead leaves and flowers promptly and remove debris.

Coral spot Although this striking fungus normally attacks dead wood on trees and shrubs, it can move to living tissue if prompt action isn't taken. Cut out dead and damaged wood and destroy infected parts.

Black spot Choose modern resistant rose varieties and break the black-spot cycle by pruning in spring, removing growth showing the shrunken black lesions, and gathering up all leaf litter in the fall.

Tidying up your garden

A well-planned, easy-care garden can be spruced up in no time, especially if lawns have been replaced by low-maintenance surfaces, and borders contain plenty of evergreens and nonflowering plants that don't need deadheading.

Garden facelift

During the growing season, weekly jobs, like mowing, deadheading, and sweeping, make a big difference to the look of the garden. Other tasks, such as hedge trimming and patio cleaning, as well as painting or refinishing various surfaces, may only be necessary once or twice a year. This "spring cleaning," however, is vital in easy-care gardens, where much more emphasis is placed on hard landscaping features. Shabby, mismatched fencing panels, peeling wall paint, faded decking, and paving slabs covered with algae catch the eye and mar your overall enjoyment. But if you have appropriate tools (some can be rented), you should be able to take care of such problem areas with ease.

Vacuum outside These handy but noisy tools allow debris, litter, and fallen leaves to be collected from paving and lawns, as well as from gravel and pebble surfaces, where it is difficult to use a brush.

Better mowing Maintain your own machine, or have it serviced regularly, to achieve the most efficient performance. Consider investing in a larger, more powerful mower if yours is too small for tackling the size of your lawn.

Keeping hedges trim Electric or gas-powered hedge trimmers are so much faster and less tiring to use than hand shears. To avoid raking up the debris, lay a tarp down to catch the trimmings.

Lift off dirt The strong jet of water produced by a pressure washer will lift grime and algae from paving, leaving a finish that looks like new. Test on a hidden corner first to make sure the surface won't be damaged.

Instant makeover Rolls of bamboo, willow, and heather screening can be used to cover mismatched fencing panels or ugly chain link for an instant and economical facelift. Attach with wire or plastic ties, or a heavy-duty staple gun.

Easy cover-up Repainting a wall freshens it up nicely, and applying a new color can add a designer touch to a patio or courtyard. After rubbing down the surface thoroughly, apply a quality exterior paint with a roller for ease.

Protect your wood Decking, fencing, trellises, and other wooden structures benefit from an application of all-weather paints, stains, and preservatives. Many companies offer special tools for speedy and efficient application.

Plant maintenance

Most of the plants in this book need very little care. Many have attractive seedheads, fruits, or stems that add interest well beyond the growing season, although some pruning or cutting back is occasionally needed to control size.

Choosing tools

Sharp, high-quality tools make light work of pruning and clipping. Always use the right size tool to avoid damaging blades when straining to cut something too thick or hard. Pruners suit many light maintenance jobs like deadheading; pruning saws are best for cutting thicker stems—loppers don't make such clean cuts.

Bypass pruners, sharpened professionally at the start of the season, tackle most pruning and deadheading jobs.

A small, curved pruning saw is invaluable for shortening thicker stems; its size and shape enable you to cut in restricted spaces.

When to prune

Generally, spring- and early summer-flowering shrubs are pruned quite lightly, immediately after flowering, to give the regrowth a chance to develop next year's flower buds. Late-summer- and fall-flowering plants, as well as many deciduous foliage shrubs, are usually pruned back relatively hard in early or mid-spring.

The late-flowering *Buddleja davidii* is cut back hard in early spring to encourage new strong growth and plentiful blooms.

Early summer-flowering shrubs, like deutzia, are pruned by cutting back stems that have flowered immediately after blooming.

To prune or not to prune?

Slow, compact, evergreen shrubs and conifers rarely need pruning, although some can be given a more formal shape by shearing them in late spring or early summer.

Deciduous shrubs and climbers, especially the more vigorous types, need some of the older wood thinned out to maintain shape and flowering potential.

Dogwoods, grown for their colorful stems, and climbers like the late-flowering viticella clematis (*above*), are pruned back hard in spring.

Shrubs and climbers rarely come to any harm if you don't get around to pruning them one year. This rambler rose thrives on neglect.

Prolonging flowering

A plant's energy and resources are used up by flower and seed production, and many stop blooming if dead or faded heads are not removed regularly. Perennials producing branched spires, such as penstemons, will often produce later flushes of blooms, if the main flower spike is removed promptly, once faded.

Knautia produces many seedheads. Instead of individual deadheading, cut the stems back now and again to encourage repeat flowering.

After the blooms of this lavender hedge have faded, use shears to cut away the flower stems and some of the current year's shoots.

Easy-care plant guide

There's a vast number of wonderful plants that will suit an easy-care garden, and here are some of the best. They are arranged in groups ranging from large trees and shrubs to low-growing ground cover, decorative perennials, and grasses. The symbols below indicate the conditions the plants prefer.

Key to plant symbols

Soil preference

⬤	Well-drained soil
◗	Moist soil
◌	Wet soil

Preference for sun or shade

☀	Full sun
◐	Partial or dappled shade
☼	Full shade

Hardiness ratings

❋ ❋ ❋	Fully hardy plants
❋ ❋	Plants that survive outside in mild regions or sheltered sites

Trees, large shrubs, and hedging

Acer palmatum 'Sango-kaku'

This elegant Japanese maple is a shade-loving deciduous tree for all seasons. In spring and fall the palmate leaves are distinctly yellow, and in winter the bright lacquer-red stems make a striking feature. Provide shelter and fertile soil.

H: 20 ft (6 m); **S**: 15 ft (5 m)
❄❄❄ ◐ ☼

Amelanchier x grandiflora 'Ballerina'

A small spreading tree for acidic, clay-rich soils and exposed sites. White blossoms smother the bare branches in spring, followed by red, ripening to black, fruits. The oval leaves, bronze-tinted in spring, color red in fall.

H: 20 ft (6 m); **S**: 25 ft (8 m)
❄❄❄ ◐ ☼ ☼

Arbutus unedo

This evergreen with flaky red-brown bark forms a large shrub or small tree in sheltered gardens. Lily-of-the-valley-like blooms appear in early winter and the rounded fruits, ripening red in fall, give rise to the common name, strawberry tree.

H: 25 ft (8 m); **S**: 25 ft (8 m)
❄❄❄ ◐ ☼

Betula utilis var. jacquemontii

For winter garden impact, plant this white-barked Himalayan birch as a multistemmed tree or a cluster of three saplings. Cultivars, including 'Jermyns' and 'Grayswood Ghost', have even brighter bark. Long catkins dangle in early spring.

H: 60 ft (18 m); **S**: 30 ft (10 m)
❄❄❄ ◐◐ ☼ ☼

Camellia x williamsii

An evergreen, shade-loving shrub that flowers through mid- and late spring and drops its spent flowers neatly. Single to fully double blooms are white through to deep pink, and cultivars are suitable for large pots or as wall shrubs. Requires acidic soil.

H: 6–15 ft (2–5 m); **S**: 3–10 ft (1–3 m)
❄❄❄ ◐ ☼

Cornus controversa 'Variegata'

Tiered whorls of branches create a distinctive architectural profile, and with bright green and white foliage and flat heads of white flowers in early summer, this charming tree makes a beautiful focal point. Requires neutral to acidic soil.

H: 23 ft (7 m); **S**: 23 ft (7 m)
❄❄❄ ◐◐ ☼ ☼

Cornus kousa *var.* chinensis *'China Girl'*
This small conical tree, for neutral to acidic soils, has tiny green flowers in early summer, surrounded by creamy-white, petal-like bracts. Fleshy red fruits develop later, followed by purple-red fall leaves.

H: 22 ft (7 m); **S**: 15 ft (5 m)
❄❄❄ ◊ ☼ ◐

Crataegus laevigata *'Paul's Scarlet'*
Like many hawthorns, this hardy tree with a long season of interest is suitable for exposed sites. 'Paul's Scarlet' has a mass of raspberry red blossom in late spring followed by a crop of red berries loved by birds.

H: 25 ft (8 m); **S**: 25 ft (8 m)
❄❄❄ ◊ ◊ ☼ ◐

Cupressus sempervirens *Stricta Group*
The narrow columns of Italian cypress act like exclamation marks. Informal groups also work well in Mediterranean-style gravel gardens, casting little shade. Maintain a single leading shoot when plants are young.

H: 70 ft (20 m); **S**: 10 ft (3 m)
❄❄❄ ◊ ☼

Fagus sylvatica
Beech makes an excellent hedge or windbreak, holding on to its coppery fall leaves through winter; the new spring foliage is bright green. Plant bareroot hedging between late fall and early spring. Trim once in late summer. Chalk tolerant.

H: 4–20 ft (1.2–6 m); **S**: 4–6 ft (1.2–2 m)
❄❄❄ ◊ ◊ ☼ ◐

Fatsia japonica
The false castor-bean plant is a shade-loving evergreen that adds a tropical or contemporary touch with its glossy, hand-shaped leaves and branched flowerheads in fall. Plant in late spring in a sheltered spot. Remove frost-damaged leaves in spring.

H: 5–12 ft (1.5–4 m); **S**: 5–12 ft (1.5–4 m)
❄❄ ◊ ◐

Ilex *x* altaclerensis *'Golden King'*
Sparkling in winter sunshine with its glossy, almost spineless, yellow-edged leaves, this holly makes a neat conical shape with little pruning. Despite its name, 'Golden King' is female and, with male pollen in the vicinity, produces crops of red berries.

H: 20 ft (6 m); **S**: 13 ft (4 m)
❄❄❄ ◊ ☼ ◐

Trees, large shrubs, and hedging

Magnolia x loebneri 'Leonard Messel'

This rounded tree or large shrub blooms on bare branches in mid-spring. The eye-catching flowers are lilac pink and produced in abundance. Provide fertile, moisture-retentive soil and shelter from wind. Tolerates lime.

H: 25 ft (8 m); **S**: 20 ft (6 m)
❊❊❊ ◐ ☼ ☼

Mahonia x media 'Charity'

As well as upright flower clusters in late fall and blue-black berries loved by birds, 'Charity' is strikingly architectural, with whorls of large, evergreen, spiny leaves. 'Winter Sun' blooms through winter. Prune lightly after flowering to keep compact.

H: 15 ft (5 m); **S**: 12 ft (4 m)
❊❊❊ ◐ ☼

Malus x robusta 'Red Sentinel'

Crab apples are two-season plants offering both blossoms and attractive fruits. 'Red Sentinel' is very hardy and bears white flowers in late spring followed by small yellow-red glossy fruits that turn dark red with age and last well into winter.

H: 22 ft (7 m); **S**: 22 ft (7 m)
❊❊❊ ◐ ☼

Photinia x fraseri 'Red Robin'

Although this evergreen can be kept fairly compact through spring and summer pruning, it makes an excellent back-of-border plant or informal hedge. The new growth is bright coppery red and large heads of tiny white flowers appear in late spring.

H: 15 ft (5 m); **S**: 15 ft (5 m)
❊❊❊ ◌ ◐ ☼ ☼

Phyllostachys nigra

Black bamboo produces a column of slender arching stems, glossy black when mature and contrasting with the light green leaves. Associate with other architectural plants or grow in a pot. Thin out weak canes from the base and cut off low side shoots.

H: 10–15 ft (3–5 m); **S**: 6–10 ft (2–3 m)
❊❊❊ ◐ ☼ ☼

Prunus x subhirtella 'Autumnalis Rosea'

Perfect for the smaller garden, this cherry bears tiny clusters of delicate, double pale pink flowers during mild periods from fall through to spring. The leaves are narrow, bronze when young, and the habit airy.

H: 25 ft (8 m); **S**: 25 ft (8 m)
❊❊❊ ◐ ☼

Rhamnus alaternus *'Argenteovariegata'*

A white-variegated form of Italian buckthorn with contrasting black stems, this dense evergreen makes a handsome wall shrub. In a sheltered spot it can also be grown freestanding, or clipped into a broad cone or dome.

H: 15 ft (5 m); **S**: 12 ft (4 m)

❄❄ ◊ ☼

Sorbus aria *'Lutescens'*

A compact, oval-headed whitebeam, the unfurling felted leaves are silvery-white, becoming light sage with white undersides. In late spring, prominent clusters of white flowers appear, followed by dark red fruits. An ideal lawn specimen. Tolerates chalk.

H: 30 ft (10 m); **S**: 25 ft (8 m)

❄❄❄ ◊ ◊ ☼ ☼

Sorbus vilmorinii

This dainty Chinese rowan eventually forms a small tree. The dark, glossy green divided leaves turn rich red-purple in fall, and late spring flowers produce drooping clusters of crimson berries, aging to pink and white. Likes deep, fertile, acidic soil.

H: 15 ft (5 m); **S**: 15 ft (5 m)

❄❄❄ ◊ ☼ ☼

Taxus baccata

Clipped as a hedge, the shade-loving common yew produces a smooth, dense finish. Cut once in late summer. Plant bare-root plants in the dormant season, ideally before Christmas, and container plants year-round. The whole plant is poisonous.

H: 6–12 ft (2–4 m); **S**: 3–5 ft (1–1.5 m)

❄❄❄ ◊ ◊ ☼ ☀

Viburnum *x bodnantense* *'Dawn'*

In frost-free periods, from late fall to spring, this upright deciduous shrub produces clusters of pink blooms with a strong scent of sweet almonds. It is happy in clay and requires little pruning. 'Deben' and 'Charles Lamont' are similar cultivars.

H: 10 ft (3 m); **S**: 6 ft (2 m)

❄❄❄ ◊ ☼ ☼

Viburnum tinus *'Eve Price'*

This compact and tough evergreen tolerates a wide range of soils and flowers from early winter to mid-spring. Flower clusters are pink in bud, opening white and honey-scented, and these are followed by blue-black berries that are attractive to birds.

H: 10 ft (3 m); **S**: 10 ft (3 m)

❄❄❄ ◊ ◊ ☼ ☼

Climbers

Clematis *'Bill MacKenzie'*
This vigorous cultivar flowers from midsummer to late fall and bears intriguing "lemon peel" blooms with dark red centers. Fluffy silver seedheads follow, and the foliage is light green and feathery. Prune stems almost to the ground in early spring.

H: 22 ft (7 m)
❄❄❄ ◐ ☼ ☀

Clematis *'Etoile Violette'*
From midsummer through to fall, violet-purple nodding blooms are produced on the new season's growth. As with all viticella clematis, prune hard in early spring to about 12 in (30 cm) from ground level, just above a pair of fat buds.

H: 15 ft (5 m)
❄❄❄ ◐ ☼ ☀

Clematis *'Markham's Pink'*
This dainty, double-flowered clematis has rose-pink blooms from spring to early summer and silvery ornamental seedheads. It is ideal for decorating a trellis, covering a low wall, or training up a shrub or small tree. Prune only to remove dead stems.

H: 8 ft (2.5 m)
❄❄❄ ◐ ☼ ☀

Clematis *'Perle d'Azur'*
Profuse in bloom, this sky-blue, small-flowered clematis shines from midsummer to fall even on a north-facing wall. Prune back to about 12 in (30 cm) from ground level in spring, just above strong buds. 'Prince Charles' is more compact.

H: 15 ft (5 m)
❄❄❄ ◐ ☼ ☀

Euonymus fortunei *'Silver Queen'*
Though usually grown as ground cover, euonymus cultivars will climb walls and fences, self-clinging via aerial roots. 'Silver Queen' makes dense, bushy wall cover, adding light to a shady view, and the white edges turn pink in winter. Trim to neaten.

H: 20 ft (6 m)
❄❄❄ ◐ ◐ ☼ ☀

Hedera helix *'Glacier'*
The gray-green, three- to five-lobed leaves of this English ivy are marbled with a variable white margin that is brightest in good light. Self-clinging stems make a close-knit wall or fence covering, and it can be pruned at any time to control spread.

H: 8 ft (2.5 m)
❄❄❄ ◐ ◐ ☼ ☀

Hydrangea anomala *subsp.* petiolaris

Although this deciduous, self-clinging climber takes a few years to begin climbing and flowering in earnest, it is a stunning sight on a shady wall when covered in its white midsummer blooms. It has yellow fall foliage.

H: 50 ft (15 m)
❋❋❋ ◑ ☼ ☀

Parthenocissus henryana

This well-behaved form of Virginia creeper develops silvery veins and red tints in partial shade but has better fall color in full sun, when the leaves turn crimson before falling. It clings to vertical surfaces via sticky-ended tendrils. Prune to control size.

H: 30 ft (10 m)
❋❋❋ ◑ ☼ ☀

Pileostegia viburnoides

An evergreen, self-clinging climber that thrives in sheltered sites on fertile soil. The architectural leaves are long, leathery and pointed and, in late summer and fall, frothy sprays of white flowers appear. May take a few years to reach flowering size.

H: 20 ft (6 m)
❋❋ ◊ ☼ ☀

Schizophragma integrifolium

This self-clinging, deciduous hydrangea relative blooms in midsummer and bears heads of tiny fertile flowers surrounded by showy sterile bracts. *Schizophragma hydrangeoides* 'Roseum' has pink bracts. Shade the roots and provide initial support.

H: 40 ft (12 m)
❋❋ ◑ ☼ ◐

Trachelospermum jasminoides

Confederate or star jasmine is an evergreen twining climber with small, fragrant, white pinwheel blooms in midsummer. Thrives in a hot, sheltered site. Provide wire supports. Growth may be slow at first. *Trachelospermum asiaticum* is similar.

H: 28 ft (9 m)
❋❋ ◊ ☼

Vitus vinifera 'Purpurea'

The leaves of this deciduous vine are intricately cut and a rich red-purple shade, becoming darker in fall when clusters of unpalatable small, round, purple grapes ripen. Provide support for the tendrils to cling to and plant on fertile soil.

H: 22 ft (7 m)
❋❋❋ ◊ ◑ ☼

Medium-sized shrubs

Acer palmatum *var.* **dissectum**
Dissectum Atropurpureum Group
Purple-red, finely cut foliage, which
turns a vibrant red in fall, covers the
arching stems of this slow-growing
deciduous shrub. Like other Japanese
maples, it prefers rich, moisture-
retentive soil and a sheltered site.

H: 6 ft (2 m); **S**: 10 ft (3 m)
❄❄❄ ◌ ◌ ☼ ☼

Aucuba japonica *'Variegata'*
Spotted laurel is a shade-loving
evergreen whose gold-splashed leaves
lighten gloomy corners. Tolerant of
pollution, it is ideal for city gardens.
Female forms, like 'Crotonifolia' and
'Variegata', have bright red berries.
Remove frost-damaged tips in spring.

H: 10 ft (3 m); **S**: 10 ft (3 m)
❄❄❄ ◌ ◌ ◌ ☼

Buddleja *'Lochinch'*
This butterfly bush has silvery-white
stems and gray-green leaves that
make a lovely foil for the pale
lavender flowerheads, which appear
from mid- to late summer. Each tiny
bloom has an orange "eye." Prune
back hard in early spring.

H: 8 ft (2.5 m); **S**: 10 ft (3 m)
❄❄❄ ◌ ☼

Ceanothus *x* **delileanus**
'Gloire de Versailles'
A deciduous California lilac, this
bushy shrub flowers prolifically from
midsummer to mid-fall. The blooms
are a soft powder-blue and work well
in a mixed border. Prune to a low
framework in mid-spring.

H: 5 ft (1.5 m); **S**: 5 ft (1.5 m)
❄❄❄ ◌ ☼

Choisya *'Aztec Pearl'*
This rounded, evergreen Mexican
orange blossom has glossy narrow
leaves that produce an airy effect.
Flowering abundantly in late spring,
with a second late-summer show,
its star-shaped blooms are pink-tinged
white and fragrant.

H: 8 ft (2.5 m); **S**: 8 ft (2.5 m)
❄❄❄ ◌ ◌ ☼ ☼

Choisya ternata *Sundance*
Lime-colored and slow-growing,
this popular, neat evergreen makes a
vibrant addition to a shady border; it
rarely flowers. On drier soils or in full
sun, the foliage is golden. Avoid poor
soils, and frost-prone or exposed
sites. A good container plant.

H: 8 ft (2.5 m); **S**: 8 ft (2.5 m)
❄❄❄ ◌ ◌ ☼ ☼

Cornus alba *'Sibirica'*
This slowly suckering dogwood has red fall foliage and lacquer-red winter stems. Plant in groups for maximum impact, and prune hard in early spring to promote plenty of new growth with vibrant color. Tolerates waterlogged clay.

H: 10 ft (3 m); **S**: 10 ft (3 m)
❋❋❋ ◗◖◗ ☼ ☀

Cornus alba *'Spaethii'*
Variegated dogwoods provide foliage contrast in mixed borders and help to lighten evergreen plantings. When established, prune out one-third of the oldest growth in early spring to promote the cherry-red winter stems. Remove all-green shoots.

H: 10 ft (3 m); **S**: 10 ft (3 m)
❋❋❋ ◗◖◗ ☼ ☀

Daphne bholua *'Jacqueline Postill'*
This late-winter-flowering evergreen daphne is hard to beat for fragrance, especially when planted in a spot sheltered from wind. The small but numerous blooms are deep purple-pink outside and white within. Mulch to retain moisture.

H: 6–12 ft (2–4 m); **S**: 5 ft (1.5 m)
❋❋❋ ◗ ☼ ☀

Escallonia laevis *'Gold Brian'*
This compact cultivar is grown mainly for its attractive bright, lime-green to gold, glossy foliage. A reliable evergreen for most gardens, it resents exposure to cold, drying winds. Deep pink blooms are produced during summer. Pruning is rarely required.

H: 4 ft (1.2 m); **S**: 4 ft (1.2 m)
❋❋❋ ◖◗ ☼ ☀

Fargesia murielae *'Simba'*
An excellent dwarf form of bamboo, 'Simba' is well behaved either in the border or in a large container. The fluttering leaves clothing the upright stems are a fresh, light green. Thin out weak stems, and some older than three years, to maintain an airy habit.

H: 6 ft (2 m); **S**: 24 in (60 cm)
❋❋❋ ◗ ☼ ☀

Hebe *'Great Orme'*
A long-flowering hebe with tapering, rich pink, fading to white blooms from midsummer to fall. The stems are purple, contrasting attractively with the narrow, glossy, mid-green leaves. Ideal for city or seaside gardens with shelter from cold winds.

H: 4 ft (1.2 m); **S**: 4 ft (1.2 m)
❋❋ ◗ ☼

Medium-sized shrubs

Hebe salicifolia
A hardy species, this narrow-leaved hebe flowers between early summer and mid-fall. Tapering white or lilac-tinged blooms are borne on upright to arching stems clothed in light green leaves. *Hebe* 'Spender's Seedling' is similar but more compact.

H: 8 ft (2.5 m); **S**: 8 ft (2.5 m)
❋❋❋ ◌ ☼

Hydrangea arborescens *'Annabelle'*
The blooms of this long-flowering American hydrangea first appear in early summer; they are fresh apple-green in bud, expanding to form very large creamy-white domes. They then make attractive papery heads in fall. Prune lightly in spring.

H: 8 ft (2.5 m); **S**: 8 ft (2.5 m)
❋❋❋ ◑ ☼ ☼

Hydrangea paniculata
With abundant cone-shaped creamy-white heads in late summer, forms of *H. paniculata* are ideal for the mixed border; pink tints often develop in fall, especially in cultivars like 'Unique'. Prune to a low framework each spring for larger blooms.

H: 10 ft (3 m); **S**: 8 ft (2.5 m)
❋❋❋ ◑ ☼ ☼

Hydrangea *'Preziosa'*
This compact hydrangea has dark mahogany stems and red fall tints. Late-summer flowers beautifully combine young, pale pink blooms with mature heads of deep red, tinted purple in acidic soil. Trim shoot tips to the first fat buds in spring.

H: 5 ft (1.5 m); **S**: 5 ft (1.5 m)
❋❋ ◑ ☼ ☼

Hydrangea serrata *'Bluebird'*
A lacecap type with narrow, tapered leaves, this dainty hydrangea bears porcelain-blue heads over a long period through summer into fall. 'Grayswood', with mauve blooms, acquiring raspberry tints in fall, is slightly taller at 6 ft (2 m).

H: 4 ft (1.2 m); **S**: 4 ft (1.2 m)
❋❋ ◑ ☼ ☼

Juniperus x pfitzeriana *'Sulphur Spray'*
The arching to upright branches of this juniper are covered in feathery sprays of pale sulfur-tinted foliage, the coloring most pronounced at the shoot tips. Stems may be removed to control height and spread.

H: 5 ft (1.5 m); **S**: 5 ft (1.5 m)
❋❋❋ ◌ ◑ ☼

Nandina domestica

Heavenly bamboo is an evergreen or semievergreen shrub with upright stems. The divided leaves are tinted coppery red when young and develop strong red-purple tones in winter. Midsummer flower sprays are white, developing into orange-red berries.

H: 6 ft (2 m); **S**: 5 ft (1.5 m)
❄❄ ◊ ☀

Olearia x haastii

This small-leaved evergreen is neat and compact and thrives in sheltered urban gardens or in seaside areas. The leathery leaves have a white felted reverse. Frothy heads of tiny white, yellow-centered daisies appear between mid- and late summer.

H: 6 ft (2 m); **S**: 10 ft (3 m)
❄❄ ◊ ☀

Osmanthus x burkwoodii

In mid-spring this small-leaved evergreen is smothered in clusters of tiny white tubular blooms with a strong perfume. A compact shrub, it doesn't require pruning but can be clipped immediately after flowering to form simple topiary shapes.

H: 10 ft (3 m); **S**: 10 ft (3 m)
❄❄❄ ◊◑ ☀ ◐

Phormium 'Alison Blackman'

A New Zealand flax with olive-green-centered leaves carrying gold stripes with a narrow red margin. Tall flower shoots sometimes appear in summer. Tougher than many other colored-leaf cultivars. 'Sundowner' has similar coloring but is larger.

H: 4½ ft (1.4 m); **S**: 4½ ft (1.4 m)
❄❄ ◊◑ ☀

Phormium tenax Purpureum Group

Ideal for a dramatic focal point in the border, members of this group have tapering, strap-shaped leaves that arch at the tip and, when mature, produce towering, rodlike flower stems. The cultivars 'Platt's Black' and 'All Black' are particularly dark.

H: 6 ft (2 m); **S**: 8 ft (2.5 m)
❄❄ ◊◑ ☀

Physocarpus opulifolius 'Diabolo'

Use this dark-purple-leaved form of the deciduous ninebark for foliage contrast in the mixed border. The leaves are trilobed and toothed, and in early summer dome-shaped heads of pale pink blooms appear. Spring-prune for larger leaves.

H: 6–8 ft (2–2.5 m); **S**: 8 ft (2.5 m)
❄❄❄ ◊◑ ☀ ◐

Medium-sized shrubs

Pittosporum 'Garnettii'
These New Zealand natives make useful evergreen backdrops or wall shrubs for sheltered town gardens and seaside plots. 'Garnettii' has mahogany stems with gray-green, white-edged leaves, pink-tinged in winter, and dark purple, scented spring blooms.

H: 10 ft (3 m); **S**: 6 ft (2 m)
❉❉ ◊ ☼

Rhododendron yakushimanum
An evergreen for acidic soil that makes a neat dome shape. It produces rose-pink buds in spring that open to large heads of white and pale pink bell-shaped blooms. The new leaf growth, covered in a colorful felting of light cinnamon, is also a feature.

H: 6 ft (2 m); **S**: 6 ft (2 m)
❉❉❉ ◐ ☼ ☼

Rosa glauca
Even when not in flower, this shrub rose makes an attractive foil for flowers in the mixed border. Arching red-purple stems bear soft purple-gray leaves and, in summer, single cerise-tinted blooms appear, later producing dark red spherical hips.

H: 6 ft (2 m); **S**: 5 ft (1.5 m)
❉❉❉ ◊ ◐ ☼ ☼

Rosa rugosa 'Alba'
A shrub rose with apple-green, virtually disease-free foliage and yellow fall color. All summer, flushes of large, single, fragrant white blooms appear, each with a yellow eye. Showy tomato-red hips follow, which are attractive to finches.

H: 6 ft (2 m); **S**: 6 ft (2 m)
❉❉❉ ◐ ☼ ☼

Sambucus nigra 'Black Lace' (syn. 'Eva')
Aptly named, this deciduous elderberry has finely-cut, purple-black foliage and, if only lightly pruned, flat plates of pink summer blossoms and black berries. Prune to a low framework in early spring to keep compact.

H: 10 ft (3 m); **S**: 10 ft (3 m)
❉❉❉ ◐ ☼ ☼

Sarcococca hookeriana var. digyna
The upright stems of this suckering evergreen shrub are clothed in shiny, narrow, tapering leaves. In winter, tiny blooms with tufts of cream anthers release a pervasive perfume, giving rise to the common name of sweet box. Shiny black berries follow.

H: 5 ft (1.5 m); **S**: 6 ft (2 m)
❉❉❉ ◐ ☼ ☼

Skimmia japonica *'Rubella'*

This glossy, evergreen woodlander has showy cones of crimson flower buds that develop in fall and open to sweetly fragrant white blooms in spring. This cultivar is male, so it does not produce berries. It is slow-growing, and needs shelter and fertile soil.

H: 5 ft (1.5 m); **S**: 5 ft (1.5 m)
❋❋❋ ◊ ☼ ☀

Syringa meyeri *'Palabin'*

This dwarf lilac has fragrant, lavender-pink blooms in late spring and early summer and small oval leaves. It thrives on neutral to alkaline soils. *Syringa pubescens* subsp. *microphylla* 'Superba' flowers intermittently from spring to fall.

H: 6 ft (2 m); **S**: 5 ft (1.5 m)
❋❋❋ ◊ ◊ ☼ ☀

Taxus baccata *'Standishii'*

Ideal for lightening a shady area or as a focal point among ground cover, this golden-leaved yew makes a compact column over time. Prune back competing leading shoots to reduce spread. *Taxus baccata* 'Fastigiata Aureomarginata' is larger.

H: 5 ft (1.5 m); **S**: 24 in (60 cm)
❋❋❋ ◊ ◊ ☼ ☀

Viburnum x burkwoodii *'Anne Russell'*

In mid- and late spring this compact, deciduous viburnum produces domed heads of waxy-textured, sweetly fragrant blooms that are pink in bud, opening white. Red fruits and colorful tints feature in fall.

H: 6 ft (2 m); **S**: 5 ft (1.5 m)
❋❋❋ ◊ ☼ ☀

Viburnum davidii

This evergreen has handsome dark leaves, held on red leaf stalks, with distinctive, deeply grooved, parallel veins giving a pleated effect. Small flower clusters in late spring produce lustrous blue berries on female shrubs when both sexes are present.

H: 3 ft (1 m); **S**: 5 ft (1.5 m)
❋❋❋ ◊ ☼ ☀

Weigela florida *'Foliis Purpureis'*

The bronzy-purple foliage of this compact, deciduous weigela is its main feature. In late spring and early summer, clusters of crimson buds open to funnel-shaped blooms with pale pink interiors, and these contrast well with the dark leaves.

H: 3 ft (1 m); **S**: 5 ft (1.5 m)
❋❋❋ ◊ ☼ ☀

Low shrubs, shorter perennials, and ground-cover plants

Acorus gramineus *'Ogon'*
This variegated Japanese rush produces fans of grassy foliage with bold gold and green stripes. Often grown as a marginal plant in ponds, this variety also thrives on fertile, moisture-retentive soil and makes an excellent foliage container plant.

H: 10 in (25 cm); **S**: 6 in (15 cm)
❄❄❄ ◐◖ ☼ ◑

Anaphalis triplinervis *'Sommerschnee'*
Pearly everlasting is a clump-forming perennial with felted, gray-green, lance-shaped leaves. From mid-to late summer it bears ball-shaped flowers made of pure white papery bracts. Avoid very dry soil in summer.

H: 28 in (70 cm); **S**: 24 in (60 cm)
❄❄❄ ◇◐◖ ☼ ◑

Armeria maritima
Varieties of sea pink or thrift are drought-tolerant evergreens that make fine grassy tussocks. The abundant white, pink, or red-purple flowers of *A. maritima* are borne in spherical clusters between late spring and early summer.

H: 8 in (20 cm); **S**: 12 in (30 cm)
❄❄❄ ◇ ☼

Artemisia schmidtiana *'Nana'*
Both the species and the dwarf form 'Nana' create low domes of bright, silvery-green, filigree foliage. Close-planted to form an evergreen carpet, they are ideal as drought-tolerant ground cover or to front a dry border. The flowers are insignificant.

H: 3 in (8 cm); **S**: 12 in (30 cm)
❄❄❄ ◇ ☼

Artemisia stelleriana *'Boughton Silver'*
The white-felted foliage of this low evergreen is intricately cut and looks more like lace than leaves. Use it to fill gaps between other plants, especially toward the front of the border, or to provide textural contrast in a container.

H: 6 in (15 cm); **S**: 18 in (45 cm)
❄❄❄ ◇ ☼

Arum italicum *'Marmoratum'*
From late fall through to mid-spring, the marbled, arrow-shaped leaves of lords and ladies cover the ground. In spring, pale green flowers appear, followed by gleaming spikes of fall berries. Good on heavier soils, it needs moisture in sunshine.

H: 12 in (30 cm); **S**: 6 in (15 cm)
❄❄❄ ◖ ☼ ●

Astilbe *'Bronce Elegans'*
This pretty, dwarf astilbe has finely cut, rich copper foliage in spring and feathery pink plumes from mid- to late summer. Plants form creeping herbaceous colonies and are suitable for the front of a border. Tolerates full sun given plentiful moisture.

H: 12 in (30 cm); **S**: 10 in (25 cm)
❄❄❄ ◐◗ ☼ ☀

Bergenia cordifolia *'Purpurea'*
This evergreen elephant's-ears has magenta bell-shaped flowers in late winter and rich purple-red leaf tones through fall and winter. Its large, glossy, rounded leaves make a strong contrast with grassy foliage plants. *Bergenia purpurascens* is similar.

H: 24 in (60 cm); **S**: 30 in (75 cm)
❄❄❄ ◐ ☼ ☀

Carex flagellifera
One of the New Zealand sedges, this evergreen has upright then arching clumps of fine wiry foliage, tinted gingery-brown. Plant singly to accent low creepers, or in multiples for ground cover with a contemporary look. *Carex testacea* is similar.

H: 3½ ft (1.1 m); **S**: 36 in (90 cm)
❄❄❄ ◐ ☼ ☀

Carex oshimensis *'Evergold'*
This bright, gold and green-striped evergreen sedge from Japan makes hummocks of narrow, arching, grassy leaves. Planted in groups it provides colorful ground cover, but it also works well in containers. Remove or trim brown leaves in spring.

H: 12 in (30 cm); **S**: 14 in (35 cm)
❄❄❄ ◐ ☼ ☀

Ceratostigma plumbaginoides
This creeping plant attracts the eye in late summer when the red stems are studded with gentian-blue blooms. In fall, the carpet of bright green leaves turn red or purple, providing a striking foil for the remaining flowers. Avoid very poor dry soils.

H: 18 in (45 cm); **S**: 12 in (30 cm)
❄❄❄ ◌◐ ☼

Cistus x dansereaui *'Decumbens'*
From late spring to midsummer, this rock rose produces a succession of pure white, tissue-paper blooms marked with maroon blotches. The sticky evergreen foliage makes fine ground cover for banks and hot, dry borders. *Cistus x hybridus* is similar.

H: 24 in (60 cm); **S**: 36 in (90 cm)
❄❄ ◌ ☼

Low shrubs, shorter perennials, and ground-cover plants

Cistus x lenis 'Grayswood Pink'
Blooming in summer, this pretty pink-flowered rock rose is one of the hardiest in cultivation. Low-growing, it spreads to cover a large area, sometimes rooting where the stems touch the ground. Useful for gravel gardens, walls, and banks.

H: 12 in (30 cm); **S**: 10 ft (3 m)
❄❄❄ ◊ ☀

Convolvulus cneorum
With leaves like strips of silvery metal, this compact, dome-shaped evergreen gleams in sunshine. Starting in spring, flushes of pink buds open to white funnel-shaped blooms. Thrives in shelter in poor, slightly alkaline soil with sharp winter drainage.

H: 24 in (60 cm); **S**: 36 in (90 cm)
❄❄ ◊ ☀

Cotoneaster horizontalis
This tough, deciduous shrub produces a herringbone pattern of branches clothed in small, glossy, dark green leaves that turn red in fall. In late spring, it is smothered in tiny blossoms that ripen to long-lasting red berries. It makes good ground or wall cover.

H: 4 ft (1.2 m); **S**: 5 ft (1.5 m)
❄❄❄ ◊ ◊ ☀ ◐

Cyclamen hederifolium
Carpets of this self-seeding cyclamen steadily build up under established trees and shrubs, thriving in soil rich in leafmold. The delicate pink blooms appear in fall before the marbled, arrow-shaped leaves, which last throughout winter and spring.

H: 5 in (13 cm); **S**: 6 in (15 cm)
❄❄❄❄ ◊ ◐

Diascia barberae 'Blackthorn Apricot'
Providing summer-flowering ground cover in well-drained gardens, several diascias are hardy, especially the brick-pink 'Ruby Field' , but need plentiful summer moisture. Clip over in spring. They overwinter best in containers.

H: 10 in (25 cm); **S**: 20 in (50 cm)
❄❄ ◊ ☀

Dicentra 'Stuart Boothman'
This low-growing bleeding heart has feathery blue-gray foliage and, from mid-spring to late summer, arching sprays of deep pink blooms. It prefers fertile, moisture-retentive soil, conditions that prolong both flowering and foliage displays.

H: 12 in (30 cm); **S**: 16 in (40 cm)
❄❄❄ ◊ ◐

Erica carnea *'Springwood White'*
Between midwinter and mid-spring, the carpet of emerald-green foliage is covered in tiny, white, honey-scented flowers that attract early bees. It has a trailing habit. Another excellent white is *Erica* x *darleyensis* 'Silberschmelze'. Clip after flowering.

H: 6 in (15 cm); **S**: 18 in (45 cm)
❄❄❄ ◊ ◊ ☼

Erigeron karvinskianus
This dainty fleabane self-seeds freely, growing in cracks in walls and paving and forming colonies in gravel. All summer, a profusion of little daisylike blooms are produced; these mature from white through to deep pinky-purple, creating a two-tone effect.

H: 6 in (15 cm); **S**: 3 ft (1 m)
❄❄❄ ◊ ☼

Euonymus fortunei *'Emerald 'n' Gold'*
With copious gold variegation, this evergreen shrub is ideal for a winter border. As temperatures plummet, the foliage becomes pink-tinged. May be clipped to simple shapes. 'Canadale Gold' is similar but stronger growing.

H: 24 in (60 cm); **S**: 36 in (90 cm)
❄❄❄ ◊ ☼ ☼

Geranium *'Ann Folkard'*
From midsummer to mid-fall, this cranesbill's trailing stems produce vivid magenta-purple blooms, each with a prominent black eye. The deeply cut, five-lobed leaves are a bright lime green. Foliage darkens with age and in excessive shade.

H: 24 in (60 cm); **S**: 3 ft (1 m)
❄❄❄ ◊ ☼ ☼

Geranium *'Johnson's Blue'*
A firm favorite with gardeners, this light-lavender-blue-flowered cranesbill is easy to please and blooms from late spring well into summer. The dish-shaped flowers are enhanced by prominent pinky-blue centers. G. 'Rozanne' is longer in bloom.

H: 18 in (45 cm); **S**: 30 in (75 cm)
❄❄❄ ◊ ☼ ☼

Geranium sanguineum
The bloody cranesbill forms neat hummocks of finely cut leaves and bears small magenta-pink flowers for many weeks in summer. Ideal for gravel gardens and raised beds, it also provides good fall color. 'Album' is white-flowered.

H: 8 in (20 cm); **S**: 12 in (30 cm)
❄❄❄ ◊ ◊ ☼ ☼

Low shrubs, shorter perennials, and ground-cover plants

Hakonechloa macra *'Aureola'*

The arching, ribbonlike leaves of this Japanese grass are striped yellow and lime green, developing red tints in full sun, and becoming greener in deep shade. Best on slightly acidic soil and excellent in containers. Cut back foliage in spring.

H: 14 in (35 cm); **S**: 16 in (40 cm)
❄❄❄ ◗ ☼ ☀

Hebe cupressoides *'Boughton Dome'*

A remarkably hardy, neat evergreen with gray-green foliage in the form of overlapping scales. The domed shape contrasts well with narrow-leaved ground cover; or plant it in groups to create a repeating pattern.

H: 12 in (30 cm); **S**: 24 in (60 cm)
❄❄❄ ◊ ☼

Hebe *'Red Edge'*

The gray-green leaves of this small-leaved, hardy hebe are edged with a fine red line and become red-tinged in winter. Small, lilac-blue flowers appear in summer, unless plants have been clipped over in late spring to enhance the domed form.

H: 18 in (45 cm); **S**: 24 in (60 cm)
❄❄❄ ◊ ☼

Hedera helix *'Parsley Crested'*

Non-variegated ivies are useful for covering the dry ground beneath trees, or for making a lawn substitute surrounded by paving. 'Parsley Crested' has mid-green leaves with an undulating margin. 'Manda's Crested' is similar but copper-tinted in winter.

H: 8 in (20 cm); **S**: 6 ft (2 m)
❄❄❄ ◊ ◗ ☼ ☀

Hedera helix *'Little Diamond'*

An aptly named ivy, perfect for the front of a border or edging a container. The small, diamond-shaped leaves are marbled gray-green with a creamy-white edge. A compact, slow-growing plant, it provides dense, bushy cover.

H: 3 in (8 cm); **S**: 12 in (30 cm)
❄❄❄ ◊ ◗ ☼ ☀

Helleborus x hybridus

This group of mostly evergreen perennials flowers from midwinter to mid-spring in colors from white, through pinks and reds, to dark maroon. Centers are usually speckled. Remove withered foliage. Prefers heavy, fertile, moisture-retentive soil.

H: 18 in (45 cm); **S**: 18 in (45 cm)
❄❄❄ ◗ ◗ ☼ ☀

Heuchera *'Plum Pudding'*
A compact evergreen perennial with heart-shaped, lobed leaves colored red-purple with deeper veining. From late spring, dark wiry stems carry tiny white flowers. 'Pewter Moon' has purple leaves overlaid with silver. Susceptible to vine weevil.

H: 16 in (40 cm); **S**: 12 in (30 cm)
❄❄❄ ◊ ☼ ☼

Hosta *'Halcyon'*
An elegant hosta with tapered, slug-resistant, gray-blue leaves and soft lavender summer flowers. The blue hostas 'Krossa Regal' and 'Big Daddy', and the yellow-centred 'Great Expectations', are also slug-resistant. For added protection, grow in pots.

H: 16 in (40 cm); **S**: 28 in (70 cm)
❄❄❄ ◊ ◆ ☼ ☼

Juniperus squamata *'Blue Carpet'*
This blue-leaved conifer makes a dense evergreen, weed-suppressing carpet and ultimately needs room to spread. It tolerates thin, chalky soils and requires minimal care, but may be pruned to control its spread by cutting out whole branches.

H: 12 in (30 cm); **S**: 6 ft (2 m)
❄❄❄ ◊ ◊ ☼

Lavandula angustifolia *'Hidcote'*
One of the best dwarf lavenders, 'Hidcote' makes mounds of silvery gray leaves topped in midsummer by dark purple spikes. To keep plants bushy and well clothed in foliage, clip over with shears after flowering. 'Munstead' is similar but paler.

H: 24 in (60 cm); **S**: 30 in (75 cm)
❄❄❄ ◊ ☼

Leucothoe *Scarletta* (syn. *'Zeblid'*)
This member of the heather family has small, glossy, evergreen leaves that turn a rich bronze red in fall, and it produces equally colorful new foliage. It requires fertile, acidic, moisture-retentive soil and shelter from wind. A good container plant.

H: 24 in (60 cm); **S**: 3½ ft (1.1 m)
❄❄❄ ◊ ☼

Libertia peregrinans
A slow-spreading grassy evergreen from New Zealand with amber-tinged foliage that brightens in winter, and white, starry spring blooms. The warm-brown-leaved 'Taupo Sunset' is an eye-catching newcomer with contrasting white flowers.

H: 20 in (50 cm); **S**: 20 in (50 cm)
❄❄ ◊ ◊ ☼ ☼

Low shrubs, shorter perennials, and ground-cover plants

Liriope muscari
Lilyturf is a hard-working evergreen perennial that makes a slow-spreading tuft of narrow, leathery, strap-shaped leaves. In late summer, long-lasting spikes of violet-purple flowers emerge. Good as fall-interest path edging or shady ground cover.

H: 12 in (30 cm); **S**: 18 in (45 cm)
❄❄❄ ◊ ◖ ☼ ◐ ☀

Muscari armeniacum
Grape hyacinth flowers in mid-spring, attracting early bees with its honey-scented blooms. The dense spikes of blue flowers emerge through grassy carpets. Unusually, this bulb's leaves appear in late summer and last until late spring. 'Blue Spike' is a double.

H: 8 in (20 cm); **S**: 2 in (5 cm)
❄❄❄ ◊ ☼ ◐

Narcissus *'February Gold'*
Dwarf, cyclamineus daffodils are invaluable for creating early spring color, and most naturalize well in informal lawns and under trees. With the narrow foliage dying down gracefully, they are also suitable for borders, even in heavy soil.

H: 12 in (30 cm); **S**: 3 in (8 cm)
❄❄❄ ◊ ☼ ◐ ☀

Ophiopogon planiscapus *'Nigrescens'*
Black mondo grass, actually a member of the lily family, makes a spreading carpet of virtually black, strappy leaves. Tolerating a wide range of conditions, it keeps its color well even in dry shade.

H: 8 in (20 cm); **S**: 12 in (30 cm)
❄❄❄ ◊ ◖ ☼ ☀

Origanum laevigatum *'Herrenhausen'*
This pretty ornamental oregano is a drought-buster. With purple-tinged leaves and stems, it makes excellent edging. From midsummer, it produces small, rounded heads of pink blooms followed by pretty seedheads.

H: 18 in (45 cm); **S**: 18 in (45 cm)
❄❄❄ ◊ ☼

Osteospermum jucundum
This South African daisy bears long-stemmed flowers, with a darker "eye" and smoky reverse, through summer and into fall. The evergreen carpeting foliage can be used to flow over the edge of retaining walls or to soften paving on a hot, sunny patio.

H: 20 in (50 cm); **S**: 36 in (90 cm)
❄❄❄ ◊ ☼

Pachysandra terminalis *'Variegata'*
The cream-variegated form of this glossy-leaved, evergreen ground cover is slightly slower-growing than the species and useful for lightening areas in dappled shade beneath trees or shrubs. Best given shelter and acidic, moisture-retentive soil.

H: 10 in (25 cm); **S**: 24 in (60 cm)
❄❄❄ ◌ ☼ ◑

Penstemon *'Evelyn'*
Unlike most border penstemons, this evergreen, narrow-leaved perennial is compact and ideal for edging a bed or for planting in pots. The rose-pink tubular blooms continue from midsummer into fall, especially with frequent deadheading.

H: 24 in (60 cm); **S**: 12 in (30 cm)
❄❄❄ ◌ ☼

Persicaria affinis *'Superba'*
This creeping knotweed produces mini pokers of crimson-opening-to-pink blooms from midsummer to fall. The neat carpet of foliage turns brown in winter but remains attractive. Good between rocks and for fronting shrub borders.

H: 10 in (25 cm); **S**: 24 in (60 cm)
❄❄❄ ◌ ☼ ◑

Phormium *'Bronze Baby'*
A dwarf New Zealand flax, this cultivar has deep purple, arching, strap-shaped leaves that form bold tufts among low-growing plants. It is also excellent for providing height in containers. Protect from sharp frost with a thick mulch of bark.

H: 32 in (80 cm); **S**: 32 in (80 cm)
❄❄ ◌ ◌ ☼

Pieris japonica *'Purity'*
Many varieties of *Pieris japonica* are compact and ideal for urban gardens. 'Purity' produces upright sprays of white, lily-of-the-valley flowers in spring and pale green new leaves in whorls at the shoot tips. Provide acidic soil and avoid frosty sites.

H: 36 in (90 cm); **S**: 36 in (90 cm)
❄❄❄ ◌ ☼ ◑

Pinus mugo *'Mops'*
This slow-growing, dwarf mountain pine is almost spherical in habit, with multiple upright stems that are covered in long, evergreen, needle-like leaves. Perfect for gravel-mulched gardens with rocks and pebbles, or as specimens in containers on the patio.

H: 24 in (60 cm); **S**: 36 in (90 cm)
❄❄❄ ◌ ☼

Low shrubs, shorter perennials, and ground-cover plants

Polystichum setiferum
Divisilobum Group
This evergreen soft shield fern has highly dissected, dark green fronds with a felted texture. It makes an attractive sculptural feature in winter shade borders and containers. Remove tired fronds in spring.

H: 28 in (70 cm); **S**: 28 in (70 cm)
❄❄❄ ◊ ☼ ☀

Potentilla fruticosa
'Primrose Beauty'
Shrubby cinquefoil does well in clay, and soft-colored cultivars also enjoy partial shade. This compact, gray-green-leaved form flowers from summer to fall. Prune in spring, removing a third of the oldest stems.

H: 24 in (60 cm); **S**: 36 in (90 cm)
❄❄❄ ◊ ☼ ☀

Rhodanthemum hosmariense
Almost never out of flower, this silver-green, filigree-leaved evergreen produces most of its daisylike blooms from early to late summer. Use it to soften the edge of a sunny retaining wall, or in gaps in paving, and in poor, stony soil.

H: 12 in (30 cm); **S**: 12 in (30 cm)
❄❄❄ ◊ ☼

Rhododendron *'Vuyk's Scarlet'*
This dwarf evergreen has a low profile, making it ideal for the front of a shrub border in acidic soil. The scarlet-tinged crimson blooms are single bells with wavy margins and are produced in abundance during mid- or late spring. Tolerates sun.

H: 30 in (75 cm); **S**: 4 ft (1.2 m)
❄❄❄ ◊ ☼ ☀

Rosa *Surrey*
One of the best of the County series, this ground-cover rose bears double pink, lightly fragrant blooms in flushes between midsummer and fall. Relatively disease-free. Cut plants back in spring with a hedge trimmer. Also try the Flower Carpet series.

H: 32 in (80 cm); **S**: 4 ft (1.2 m)
❄❄❄ ◊ ☼

Scabiosa *'Butterfly Blue'*
'Butterfly Blue', and the lilac-pink 'Pink Mist', are dainty mini scabious, flowering over a long period through summer into fall, especially if deadheaded regularly. Plant at the border edge or in containers. The flowers attract bees and butterflies.

H: 16 in (40 cm); **S**: 16 in (40 cm)
❄❄❄ ◊ ☼

Sedum *'Ruby Glow'*
Carpeting stonecrops, like 'Ruby Glow' and 'Vera Jameson', combine dusky purple-tinged succulent leaves with crimson flowerheads that appear from midsummer to fall. Effective *en masse* in gravel gardens. Drought-resistant and attractive to butterflies.

H: 10 in (25 cm); **S**: 18 in (45 cm)
❄❄❄ ◊ ☼ ☼

Sempervivum tectorum
Common houseleek, also named hen-and-chicks as the rosettes of leaves are surrounded by offshoots, bears upright, red-purple flower stems in summer; the leaves may also be red-tinted. These evergreen succulents are used for living roofs.

H: 6 in (15 cm); **S**: 20 in (50 cm)
❄❄❄ ◊ ☼

Sisyrinchium striatum *'Aunt May'*
This cultivar produces white-striped evergreen leaf fans from which upright stems of creamy flowers arise in summer. Architectural in character, they work well planted in swaths in gravel gardens. Deadhead to prevent seeding.

H: 20 in (50 cm); **S**: 10 in (25 cm)
❄❄❄ ◊ ☼

Stipa tenuissima
Although this diaphanous grass makes a good pot specimen, it works best weaving through borders or planted in clumps near paving. It bears pale, biscuit-colored flower stems through summer, and the light green leaves fade but remain attractive all winter.

H: 24 in (60 cm); **S**: 12 in (30 cm)
❄❄❄ ◊ ☼

Yucca filamentosa *'Bright Edge'*
This brightly variegated form of Adam's needle is best planted as a single specimen or in small groups mulched with gravel or pebbles. Spires of creamy bells may appear in summer, but this is chiefly an evergreen foliage plant. Makes a fine container specimen.

H: 30 in (75 cm); **S**: 4 ft (1.4 m)
❄❄❄ ◊ ☼

Yucca flaccida *'Ivory'*
These architectural evergreens can be temperamental about blooming, but 'Ivory' produces its exotic-looking flowers freely. In summer, tall stems bearing a profusion of green-tinted cream bells rise from the basal rosette of blue-green, swordlike leaves.

H: 22 in (55 cm); **S**: 5 ft (1.5 m)
❄❄❄ ◊ ☼

Perennials and ornamental grasses

Acanthus spinosus
This statuesque perennial sends up glossy leaves in early spring that expand to form a mound of deeply toothed blades armed with spines. In early summer, spires of white-hooded blooms with long-lasting purple bracts appear. A paving or gravel specimen.

H: 4½ ft (1.4 m); **S**: 36 in (90 cm)
❄❄❄ ◊ ◊ ☼ ☼

Agapanthus 'Loch Hope'
This Nile lily has clumps of strap-shaped leaves and tall stems topped with striking round heads of deep blue flowers. Combining well with hot-colored blooms, they brighten flagging displays in late summer and early fall. Mulch in winter.

H: 4 ft (1.2 m); **S**: 24 in (60 cm)
❄❄❄ ◊ ◊ ☼

Allium hollandicum 'Purple Sensation'
In early summer, this ornamental onion bears drumstick heads of rich purple above a tuft of gray-green leaves. The sculptural seedheads are long-lasting and good for drying, but seedlings will produce paler blooms.

H: 3 ft (1 m); **S**: 3 in (7 cm)
❄❄❄ ◊ ☼ ☼

Anemanthele lessoniana
The pheasant's-tail grass, formerly *Stipa arundinacea*, makes a dense clump of narrow, ribbonlike foliage. Arching purple-tinted flower stems reach almost to the ground and, from fall through winter, the olive leaves are tinted orange and red.

H: 36 in (90 cm); **S**: 4 ft (1.2 m)
❄❄❄ ◊ ◊ ☼ ☼

Anemone hupehensis 'Hadspen Abundance'
An upright, free-flowering perennial that bears unevenly shaped, deep pink blooms with golden stamens from mid- to late summer. The vine-like leaves form substantial clumps. Also try *Anemone* x *hybrida* cultivars.

H: 36 in (90 cm); **S**: 16 in (40 cm)
❄❄❄ ◊ ☼ ☼

Aster x frikartii 'Mönch'
Superior to most Michaelmas daisies, this adaptable lavender-blue aster blooms from midsummer to fall. It doesn't usually need staking and has good mildew resistance. Working well with most color schemes, it is also charming with ornamental grasses.

H: 28 in (70 cm); **S**: 16 in (40 cm)
❄❄❄ ◊ ☼ ☼

Astrantia *'Hadspen Blood'*

This easy-care perennial colonizes wilder parts of the garden in dappled shade but is just as valuable in the early- and midsummer border. The dark red blooms are like tiny posies surrounded by papery bracts, and the leaves are attractively lobed.

H: 36 in (90 cm); **S**: 18 in (45 cm)
❋❋❋ ◊ ☼ ☀

Calamagrostis *x* acutiflora

A strikingly erect grass with a strong winter presence. Popular cultivars include the arching, cream-striped 'Overdam' and the taller 'Karl Foerster', which in midsummer bears pinkish-brown plumes. In fall, both take on bronze or biscuit tones.

H: 5 ft (1.5 m); **S**: 24 in (60 cm)
❋❋❋ ◊ ☼ ☀

Centranthus ruber

The red valerian, common in seaside areas, is a drought-tolerant, fleshy-leaved self-seeder that blooms from late spring to late summer. The cone-shaped crimson flower clusters are great butterfly attractors. It benefits from deadheading. 'Albus' is white.

H: 36 in (90 cm); **S**: 36 in (90 cm)
❋❋❋ ◊ ☼

Chelone obliqua

This turtlehead is a hardy late-summer-flowering perennial that tolerates clay soil and occasional waterlogging. The upright flower stems bear curious pink blooms that open from tightly clustered buds. *Chelone leyonii* is similar but taller. Protect from slugs.

H: 24 in (60 cm); **S**: 12 in (30 cm)
❋❋❋ ◊ ◐ ☼ ☀

Deschampsia cespitosa

Varieties of the tufted hair grass, such as 'Goldschleier' (syn. 'Golden Veil'), form clumps of narrow, evergreen leaves that produce gracefully arching flower stems in early summer. The airy flowerheads catch the breeze and remain attractive well into fall.

H: 4 ft (1.2 m); **S**: 4 ft (1.2 m)
❋❋❋ ◊ ☼ ☀

Dryopteris affinis *'Cristata'*

Often referred to as the king of British ferns, this handsome cultivar has arching shuttlecocks of semi-evergreen fronds with frilled or crested tips. Surprisingly tolerant, it will withstand some sun and wind exposure. A good container plant.

H: 36 in (90 cm); **S**: 36 in (90 cm)
❋❋❋ ◊ ☼ ☀

Perennials and ornamental grasses

Echinops ritro *'Veitch's Blue'*
Globe thistles are statuesque plants with coarse, deeply-toothed leaves and spherical, macelike flowerheads that are a magnet for bees, butterflies, and moths. This cultivar produces an abundance of steely blue blooms on upright, silvery stems.

H: 4 ft (1.2 m); **S**: 18 in (45 cm)
❄❄❄ ◊ ◐ ☼ ☀

Eryngium *x* oliverianum
One of the most ornamental of the sea hollies, from midsummer this hybrid has branching stems carrying abundant thimblelike heads of metallic blue, each with an elegant spiny "ruff." Although the blooms fade, they persist into fall.

H: 36 in (90 cm); **S**: 18 in (45 cm)
❄❄❄ ◊ ☼

Euphorbia characias *'Humpty Dumpty'*
This compact, evergreen spurge blooms in spring, its chunky, acid-green flowerheads contrasting well with the gray-green foliage. Remove faded flower stems but avoid touching the sap, which may irritate the skin.

H: 24 in (60 cm); **S**: 20 in (50 cm)
❄❄❄ ◊ ☼

Helictotrichon sempervirens
Blue oat grass is evergreen and drought tolerant. In early and mid-summer, the tussocks of narrow, steely blue-gray leaves send up long stems carrying oatlike flowerheads. Use as a specimen in gravel or for massed plantings.

H: 4 ft (1.2 m); **S**: 24 in (60 cm)
❄❄❄ ◊ ☼

Hemerocallis *'Corky'*
A free-flowering daylily that blooms from early to midsummer. Slender stems with dark buds produce a succession of starry yellow blooms with brown stripes on the back of the petals. Clumps of narrow, strap-shaped leaves appear in early spring.

H: 28 in (70 cm); **S**: 16 in (40 cm)
❄❄❄ ◐ ☼ ☀

Iris foetidissima
The stinking iris (its bruised leaves can smell unpleasant) has striking orange berries that burst from large pods in fall and remain attractive for weeks against the glossy, evergreen foliage. An invaluable plant for dry shade. 'Variegata' is white-striped.

H: 36 in (90 cm); **S**: 4 ft (1.2 m)
❄❄❄ ◊ ◐ ☼ ☀

Iris sibirica *'Perry's Blue'*
Early-summer-flowering Siberian iris cultivars produce blooms in shades of blue, purple, and white and give a strongly vertical accent to the border. Their grassy foliage contrasts nicely with broadleaved plants and they have attractive seed pods.

H: 4 ft (1.2 m); **S**: 36 in (90 cm)
❋❋❋ ◐◆ ☼ ◑

Knautia macedonica
Melton pastels
This pincushion-flowered perennial bears blooms in shades of deep crimson through to pinks and purples. The loose tangle of branched stems creates a natural effect suitable for informal gardens. Deadhead regularly.

H: 4 ft (1.2 m); **S**: 20 in (50 cm)
❋❋❋ ◐ ☼

Kniphofia *'Little Maid'*
An unusual and dainty red-hot poker that forms stiff, grassy clumps from which pale green flower buds appear in late summer and early fall. These expand to form pokers of pale yellow blooms that fade to cream. Protect flower buds from slugs.

H: 24 in (60 cm); **S**: 18 in (45 cm)
❋❋❋ ◐ ☼

Leucanthemum x superbum
The ubiquitous Shasta daisy tolerates a range of situations, including heavy clay, and will even hold its own in light grass cover. The long-stemmed white flowers emerge from a clump of leathery, dark green leaves from early summer to early fall.

H: 36 in (90 cm); **S**: 24 in (60 cm)
❋❋❋ ◐ ☼ ◑

Libertia grandiflora
This architectural New Zealander produces handsome, fan-shaped tufts of olive-green leaves. In late spring and early summer, sprays of white flowers appear, followed by brown seed pods, which turn black as they mature. Mulch for winter.

H: 36 in (90 cm); **S**: 24 in (60 cm)
❋❋❋ ◐ ☼

Lilium *'Enchantment'*
An easy, clump-forming lily, this is perfect planted near the front of the border. In early summer, the upright-facing, star-shaped blooms of bold orange open to reveal black-speckled centers. Add compost to sandy soils and watch out for lily beetles.

H: 24 in (60 cm); **S**: 6 in (15 cm)
❋❋❋ ◐◆ ☼ ◑

Perennials and ornamental grasses

Miscanthus sinensis 'Kleine Silbespinne'

This compact ornamental grass with white-ribbed leaves is ideal for small gardens. In late summer, it is crowned with silky tufts of purple-tinged blooms that fade to white in fall and remain attractive into winter.

H: 4 ft (1.2 m); **S**: 36 in (90 cm)
✳✳✳ ◊ ☼ ☼

Miscanthus sinensis 'Variegatus'

Variegated with creamy-white stripes, this tall grass adds light and stature to the border. For small gardens, choose 'Morning Light', which reaches 4–5 ft (1.2–1.5 m) and has narrower blades with a fine white margin. Both bear red-brown flowers in late fall.

H: 6 ft (1.8 m); **S**: 4 ft (1.2 m)
✳✳✳ ◊ ☼ ☼

Panicum virgatum 'Heavy Metal'

The prairie switchgrasses are noted for their fall foliage tints and airy panicles. 'Heavy Metal' has upright clumps of metallic, blue-gray foliage, which begin turning yellow in fall. From late summer, plants have a halo of purple-tinged flowers.

H: 36 in (90 cm); **S**: 30 in (75 cm)
✳✳✳ ◊ ☼

Penstemon 'Schoenholzeri'

Narrow-leaved penstemons, like this free-flowering cultivar, are particularly hardy. These evergreen perennials produce a long succession of flowers from midsummer, especially if deadheaded regularly. Cut back to new leaf growth in spring.

H: 30 in (75 cm); **S**: 24 in (60 cm)
✳✳✳ ◊ ◊ ☼

Penstemon 'Stapleford Gem'

This pretty, two-tone penstemon has broad leaves and an upright habit. The newer "bird" series has produced several excellent taller cultivars, such as 'Osprey', with pink and white blooms, the striking purple 'Raven', and the reddish-purple 'Blackbird'.

H: 24 in (60 cm); **S**: 18 in (45 cm)
✳✳✳ ◊ ◊ ☼

Perovskia 'Blue Spire'

Russian sage forms a clump of gray-green, toothed leaves. In late summer, wiry, branched, white stems carry tiny clusters of violet-blue flowers. A good dry garden specimen and bee magnet. The frosty-looking stems are attractive in winter.

H: 4 ft (1.2 m); **S**: 36 in (90 cm)
✳✳✳ ◊ ☼

Phlomis russeliana
This perennial's charm comes from the way the pale yellow flowers are arranged in ball-like clusters along the upright stems. The hooded blooms reach their peak in early summer but continue until early fall. Combine with other drought-tolerant plants.

H: 36 in (90 cm); **S**: 30 in (75 cm)
❋❋❋ ◊ ☼

Rudbeckia fulgida *var.* deamii
This black-eyed Susan provides vivid late summer and fall color with its golden, daisylike blooms, each with a dark, raised center. It is happy in heavy soil and the dried flowers offer winter interest. *R. fulgida* var. *sullivantii* 'Goldsturm' is similar.

H: 24 in (60 cm); **S**: 18 in (45 cm)
❋❋❋ ● ☼ ☼

Salvia *x* superba
A hybrid sage, used most effectively in large swaths, which produces upright spires of glowing violet-purple flowers between midsummer and early fall. *S. nemorosa* 'Lubecca' and *S. verticillata* 'Purple Rain' are longer-flowering and more compact.

H: 36 in (90 cm); **S**: 18 in (45 cm)
❋❋❋ ◊ ● ☼

Sedum *'Matrona'*
This fashionably dark-leaved sedum produces domed heads of tight buds that open to pink blooms in late summer, and form attractive seedheads in fall. Both foliage and stems are a dusky purple. Divide every 3–4 years. Also try 'Herbstfreude'.

H: 24 in (60 cm); **S**: 24 in (60 cm)
❋❋❋ ◊ ☼ ☼

Stipa gigantea
Giant feather grass is an evergreen, tussock-forming species that, in summer, produces tall, arching stems with large, oatlike flowers. These are green at first, turning a glistening golden yellow with age. Excellent as a specimen or mingled with flowers.

H: 8 ft (2.5 m); **S**: 4 ft (1.2 m)
❋❋❋ ◊ ☼

Verbena bonariensis
Superb planted *en masse*, this tall-stemmed, elegant, self-seeding plant can be used toward the front of a border or beside paving. The many small, domed heads of violet flowers are produced from midsummer to fall and attract butterflies.

H: 6 ft (1.8 m); **S**: 18 in (45 cm)
❋❋ ◊ ☼

Index

D. b. 'Ruby Field' 142
D. 'Sunchimes Lilac' 108, 109
Dicentra 'Stuart Boothman'
142
digging 62, 64, 65, 119
Digitalis lutea 102, 103
diseases 96, 111, 121
disorders 119
dividers 30–3
dogwood see Cornus
drainage 10, 48, 60, 61
containers 69, 83, 106, 108
improving 41, 57, 62, 90,
92, 96, 98, 104
drought-tolerant plants 25,
26, 57, 60, 67, 90–1, 104–5,
108
Dryopteris affinis 'Cristata' 151

E

Echeveria 57
Echinops
E. ritro 92, 93
E. r. 'Veitch's Blue' 152
electricity 34, 55
Erica 16
E. carnea 'Springwood
White' 143
E. x darleyensis
'Silberschmelze' 143
Erigeron 20
E. karvinskianus 143
Eryngium x oliverianum 152
Escallonia laevis 'Gold Brian'
135
Eschscholzia 16, 17
Euonymus
E. fortunei 'Canadale Gold'
143
E. f. 'Emerald 'n' Gold' 143
E. f. 'Silver Queen' 132
Euphorbia characias 'Humpty
Dumpty' 152
exposure 26, 28, 29

F

Fagus sylvatica 129
fall border 92–3
Fallopia baldschuanica 67
Fargesia 32
F. murielae 'Simba' 135

Fatsia japonica 129
fedges 33
fences 14, 15, 28, 30, 76–7,
122, 123
ferns 18, 67, 83
see also Dryopteris;
Polystichum
fertilizer 62, 84, 116
slow-release 25, 82, 94,
106, 108, 117
fertilizing 24, 25, 27, 111,
116–17
Festuca (fescue) 16
F. glauca 'Blauglut' 90, 91
focal points 8, 9, 10, 12, 13,
15, 51, 128
foliage plantings 96–7, 106–7
formal gardens 12–13, 37, 81
foxglove see Digitalis
frost 27, 28, 29, 119

G

Galanthus (snowdrop) 67
G. nivalis 88, 89
Geranium
G. 'Ann Folkard' 143
G. 'Johnson's Blue' 143
G. 'Nimbus' 100, 101
G. 'Rozanne' 143
G. sanguineum 143
grape hyacinth see Muscari
grasses 10, 15, 18, 19, 20–1,
67, 84, 116
see also Anemanthele;
Calamagrostis;
Deschampsia; Festuca;
Helictotrichon;
Miscanthus; Panicum; Stipa
gravel 24, 35, 37, 45, 55, 143
drainage 69, 83, 104, 106, 108
laid over membrane 8, 9,
25, 35, 40–1, 70–1, 119
as mulch 84, 147
gravel gardens 16, 20, 40–1,
129, 142, 149

H

Hakonechloa macra 'Aureola'
144
hard landscaping 8–9, 14–15,
24, 26, 34–7, 122, 123

see also paths; patios
hawthorn see Crataegus
heather see Erica
Hebe
H. cupressoides 'Boughton
Dome' 144
H. 'Great Orme' 135
H. 'Red Edge' 144
H. salicifolia 136
H. 'Spender's Seedling' 136
Hedera (ivy) 18, 32, 33
H. helix 57
H. h. 'Glacier' 132
H. h. 'Little Diamond' 144
H. h. 'Manda's Crested' 144
H. h. 'Parsley Crested' 144
hedges 27, 29, 74–5, 96, 113,
122, 130
boxwood 12, 13, 37, 74
yew 32, 74, 100, 101, 131
Helichrysum italicum 94, 95
Helictotrichon sempervirens
152
Helleborus (hellebore) 67
H. x hybridus 88, 89, 144
H. orientalis subsp. guttatus
88, 89
Hemerocallis 'Corky' 152
herb border 104–5
herbs 10, 11, 48, 57, 63, 108
planting 70–1
Heuchera 18
H. 'Pewter Moon' 82, 83,
145
H. 'Plum Pudding' 145
high-maintenance pruning 66
holly see Ilex
horticultural fleece 90, 106
Hosta 10, 67, 82, 83, 116
H. 'Big Daddy' 145
H. 'Great Expectations' 145
H. 'Halcyon' 145
H. 'Krossa Regal' 145
H. sieboldiana var. elegans
98, 99
houseleek see Sempervivum
hurdles 30
Hydrangea 67, 76–7
H. anomala subsp.
petiolaris 32, 133
H. arborescens 'Annabelle'
136

H. macrophylla 66
H. paniculata 136
H. 'Preziosa' 136
H. serrata 'Bluebird' 136
H. s. 'Grayswood' 136

I

Ilex (holly) 74
I. x altaclerensis 'Golden
King' 129
Impatiens 82, 83
Iris
I. foetidissima 152
I. pseudocorus var.
bastardii 96, 97
I. sibirica 96
I. s. 'Perry's Blue' 153
irrigation 75, 113
automatic 18, 24, 25, 26,
113, 114–15
ivy see Hedera

J

Japanese gardens 15, 37
Japanese maple see Acer
Jovibarba 57
Juniperus (juniper) 67
J. x pfitzeriana 'Sulphur
Spray' 136
J. squamata 'Blue Carpet'
145

K

Knautia 125
K. macedonica 100, 101
K. m. 'Melton pastels' 153
Kniphofia 'Little Maid' 153

L

labels 66, 67
labor-intensive gardens 27
landscape fabric see weed-
suppressing membrane
landscape materials 8, 9,
34–7
Lavandula (lavender) 12, 13,
20, 21, 25, 125
L. angustifolia 'Hidcote'
108, 109, 145

Index

Acknowledgments

The publisher would like to thank the following for their kind permission to reproduce their photographs:

(Key: a-above; b-below/bottom; c-center; f-far; l-left; r-right; t-top; i-inset)

2: DK Images: Peter Anderson, Designer: Geoff Whiten/The Pavestone Garden/ Chelsea Flower Show 2006. **6-7:** Stonemarket **8:** Steven Wooster, Designers: Sarah Brodie & Faith Pewhustel/'Where For Art Thou?'/Chelsea Flower Show 2002. **9:** The Garden Collection: Torie Chugg, Designer: Jill Anderson/Hampton Court 2005 (t), Marianne Majerus Photography: Designer: Lynne Marcus (b). **10:** The Garden Collection: Liz Eddison, Designer: Bob Purnell (t), The Garden Collection: Liz Eddison (br), DK Images: Peter Anderson, Designer: Kati Crome/Tufa Tea/Chelsea Flower Show 2007 (bl). **11:** The Garden Collection: Marie O'Hara, Designer: Marney Hall/ Chelsea Flower Show 2005. **12:** Garden Picture Library: Botanica (t), GAP Photos Ltd: Clive Nichols, Designer: Stephen Woodhams (b). **13:** The Garden Collection: Jonathan Buckley, Designer: Anthony Goff (t), Garden Picture Library: Ron Sutherland, Designer: Anthony Paul (b). **14:** DK Images: Steven Wooster, Kelly's Creek/Chelsea Flower Show 2000. **15:** Clive Nichols: Designer: Liz Robertson/Hampton Court 2003 (tl), The Garden Collection: Jonathan Buckley, Designer: Paul Kelly (br), DK Images: Brian North, Designers: Marcus Barnett & Philip Nixon/The Savills Garden/ Chelsea Flower Show 2007 (c). **16:** DK Images: Peter Anderson, Designer: Heidi Harvey & Fern Alder/Full Frontal/Hampton Court Palace Flower Show 2007 (t). **17:** The Garden Collection: Jonathan Buckley, Designer: Christopher Lloyd/Great Dixter (l), DK Images: Brian North, Designer: Mark Browning/The Fleming's & Trailfinders Australian Garden/Chelsea Flower Show 2007 (br). **18:** DK Images: Peter Anderson, Designer: Geoff Whiten/The Pavestone Garden/Chelsea Flower Show 2006 (b). **19:** The Garden Collection: Liz Eddison, Designer: Reaseheath College (t), DK Images: Peter Anderson, Designers: Louise Cummins & Caroline De Lane Lea/The Suber Garden/Chelsea Flower Show 2007 (b). **20:** The Garden Collection: Nicola Stocken Tomkins (b), DK Images: Peter

Anderson, Designer: Jinny Blom/ Laurent-Perrier Garden/Chelsea Flower Show 2007 (t). **21:** The Garden Collection: Liz Eddison, Design: Butler Landscapes (t). **24:** DK Images: Brian North, Designer: Harpak Design/A City Haven/Chelsea Flower Show 2007 (t). **26:** Designer: Chris Parsons/ Hallam Garden Design (t), DK Images: Brian North, Designer: Teresa Davies, Steve Putnam & Samantha Hawkins/Moving Spaces, Moving On/Chelsea Flower Show 2007 (bc), Designer: Jinny Blom/ Laurent-Perrier Garden/Chelsea Flower Show 2007 (br). **27:** DK Images: Steve Wooster, Designers: Xa Tollemache & Jon Kellett/The Merrill Lynch Garden, Chelsea Flower Show. **30:** DK Images: Peter Anderson, Designers: Chloe Salt, Roger Bullock & Jeremy Salt/Reflective Height/Chelsea Flower Show 2006 (br). **31:** DK Images: Peter Anderson, Designer: Mike Harvey/ The Unwind Garden/Hampton Court Palace Flower Show 2007. **32:** DK Images: Peter Anderson, Designer: Gabriella Pape & Isabelle Van Groeningen/The Daily Telegraph Garden/Chelsea Flower Show 2007 (br). **33:** DK Images: Peter Anderson, Designer: Chris Beardshaw/The Chris Beardshaw Garden/Chelsea Flower Show 2007 (t). **34:** Stonemarket **35:** Stonemarket (bl) (br), DK Images: Peter Anderson, Designers: James Mason & Chloe Gazzard/ The Path Not Taken/Hampton Court Palace Flower Show 2007 (bc). **36:** The Garden Collection: Liz Eddison, Designer: Thomas Hoblyn. **37:** Stonemarket (bl), Garden Picture Library: Mark Bolton (br), DK Images: Peter Anderson, Designer: Ulf Nordfjell/A Tribute to Linnaeus/Chelsea Flower Show 2007 (tr). **38:** The Garden Collection: Nicola Stocken Tomkins, Stonemarket (i). **44:** The Garden Collection: Nicola Stocken Tomkins. **50:** DK Images: Peter Anderson, Designer: Thomas Hoblyn Garden Design/The Homebase Garden of Reflections/Hampton Court Palace Flower Show 2007. **51:** DK Images: Brian North, Designer: Adam Frost/Realistic Retreat/ Chelsea Flower Show 2007 (tl), Peter Anderson, Designer: Helen Williams/The Green & Light Garden/Hampton Court Palace Flower Show 2007 (tr), Designers: Marcus Barnett & Philip Nixon/The Savills Garden/Chelsea Flower Show 2007 (bl). **56:** Marianne Majerus Photography:

Designer: Christopher Masson (t). **57:** DK Images: Peter Anderson, Designers: Paula Ryan, Artillery Architecture & Interior Design/The Amnesty International Garden for Human Rights/Chelsea Flower Show 2007 (tl), Brian North, Designer: Mark Browning/ The Fleming's & Trailfinders Australian Garden/Chelsea Flower Show 2007 (bl). **86-87:** DK Images: Peter Anderson, Designer: Linda Bush/The Hasmead Sand & Ice Garden/Chelsea Flower Show 2007. **89:** Marianne Majerus Photography. **90-91:** DK Images: Peter Anderson, Designer: Linda Bush/ The Hasmead Sand & Ice Garden/Chelsea Flower Show 2007. **92-93:** Marianne Majerus Photography: Designers: Brita von Schoenaich & Tim Rees/Ryton Organic Garden (t). **95:** Clive Nichols: Woodpeckers, Warwickshire. **99:** Garden Picture Library: Ron Evans. **100-101:** DK Images: Peter Anderson, Designers: Laurie Chetwood & Patrick Collins/Chetwoods Urban Oasis/ Chelsea Flower Show 2007. **102:** Alamy Images: CuboImages srl (cr). **104-105:** DK Images: Peter Anderson, Designer: Scenic Blue/The Marshalls Sustainability Garden/ Chelsea Flower Show 2007.

110-111: Ronseal. **122:** Alamy Images: The Photolibrary Wales (bl). **123:** Ronseal (br), DK Images: Brian North, Designers: Harry Levy & Geoff Carter/The Water Garden/ Tatton Park 2007 (tr). **128:** Caroline Reed (tr). **133:** Caroline Reed (bc). **134:** Caroline Reed (tr). **135:** Jenny Hendy (bl). **136:** Caroline Reed (tl), Jenny Hendy (br) **138:** Caroline Reed (bc). **147:** Clive Nichols: (bc). **149:** GAP Photos Ltd: S & O (br). **150:** Alamy Images: Niall McDiarmid (br).

All other images © Dorling Kindersley. For further information see: www.dkimages.com

Dorling Kindersley would also like to thank the following:

Index: Jane Coulter

Hallam Garden Design (www.hallamgardendesign.co.uk), Stonemarket (www.stonemarket.co.uk), and Ronseal (www.ronseal.co.uk) for photographs.

Hyde Hall (www.rhs.org.uk) for photography locations.